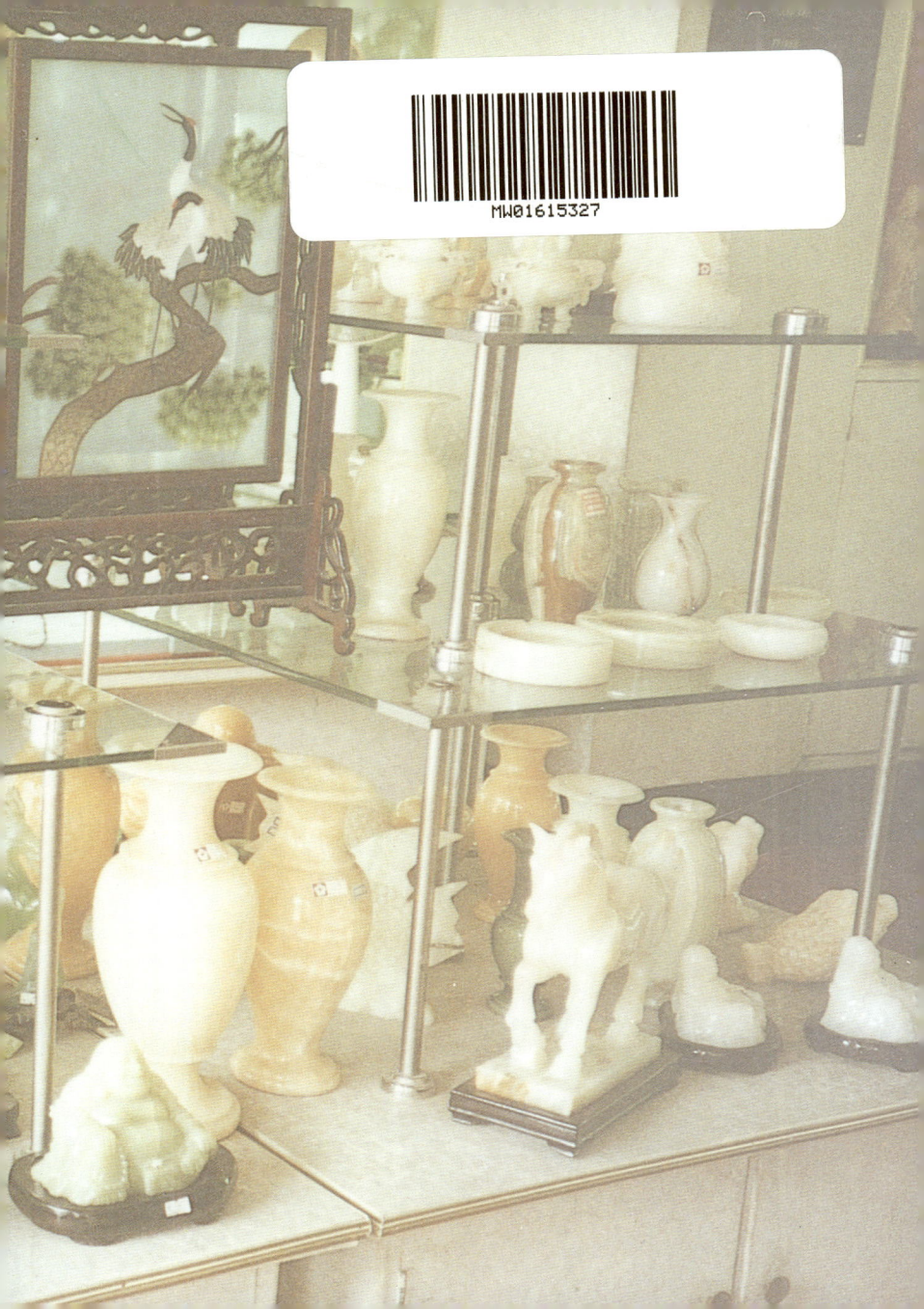

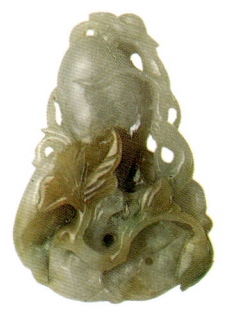

# Chinese Jade

## Power and Delicacy
## in a Majestic Art

Minghua Zhang

LONG RIVER PRESS
San Francisco

First Edition 2004
Copyright © Shanghai People's Fine Arts Publishing House (Chinese edition)
Copyright © 2004 Long River Press (English edition)
All rights reserved. No part of this book may be reproduced without written
permission of the publisher

ISBN 1-59265-011-2

**Library of Congress Cataloging-in-Publication Data**

Zhang, Minghua
[Yu qi. English]
Chinese jade : power and delicacy in a majestic art / by Zhang Minghua.—1st ed.
    p. cm.
ISBN 1-59265-011-2 (hardcover)
1. Jade art objects—China. I. Title.
NK5750.2C6 Z47 2004
736'.24'0951—dc22
                                    2004005190


Published in the United States of America by
Long River Press
3450 3rd St., #4B, San Francisco, CA 94124
www.longriverpress.com
in association with Shanghai People's Fine Arts Publishing House

Printed in China

10 9 8 7 6 5 4 3 2 1

# Table of Contents

## Introduction

$\mathcal{J}$ade has been synonymous with Chinese art for thousands of years. Some of the most treasured artistic pieces in museums throughout the world represent the finest cultural masterpieces of Chinese history. Jade has fascinated art lovers worldwide because of both its grandeur and its intimacy; the sheer variety of colors and shapes depicted make it unique as both a subject of art as well as a subject of the realm of geologic formations. This book, designed to serve as an introduction to the world of jade in China, presents some basic background information, including history, cultural significance, and importance to the overall Chinese artistic canon.

# 1. Searching for Jade

*W*hen examining a piece of raw jade, it is often difficult to associate it with an exquisite piece of carved jade art. A piece of raw jade as found in nature often does not look much different than a common pebble or rough stone. Once, there was a man named Bian He, who lived in the ancient State of Chu (ca. 1100-221 BC), who presented a piece of unpolished jade to the king only to be punished by having feet chopped off. It is a simple explanation of how the real value of a piece of jade could not easily be recognized.

Jade stones as natural components of geologic formations cannot be randomly mined. The process of removing deposits of jade requires considerable expertise and deft handling to extract them correctly, especially so when large jade formations are encountered. Before the Qing Dynasty (1644-1911), large pieces of jade rocks were very rare.

A masterpiece of Chinese art entitled *Great Yu Taming the Flood*, is carved from a single piece of jade weighing 5.8 tons, and sourced from the Mierdai Mountains in the Xinjiang area of northwest China. Generally speaking, jade mined from mountains rarely produces artistic works of high-quality. Rather, the appeal of mountain jade is often its huge quantity. Large-size jade carvings are almost always made out of mountain jade. A closer look at *Great Yu Taming the Flood* clearly reveals the presence of stone veins which spread out over the entire piece.

Another type of raw jade can be found in the rivers and streams flowing out of mountainous regions. Smaller in size, such jade stones give the impression of being soft-surfaced, while others may have sharp angles which can produce top-quality jade ware. As these stones lie in the upper reaches of the river near their origins in the mountains, they are relatively easy to extract once the water level is low.

The last category of jade comes from riverbeds away from

mountains or in what once were prehistoric flood plains. Enduring countless years of erosion, they were corroded and dyed by mineral deposits, displaying a yellowish gray or red or purple surface, known as "water rust skin." When the corrosive mineral deposits are removed, the original color of the stones is restored, and these are known as "tiger skin stones." These stones, washed by water and ground by sand, almost have no sharp angles on their surface. They resemble ordinary river pebbles.

In *Tales from the Western Regions*, written during the Qing Dynasty, jade originating from the Hotan area of the Xinjiang region is described thusly: "Here river jade stones are as large as grinding stones and as small as chestnuts. They can be pure white, green, yellow or red, but the dark colored stones are the most valuable. Some can be as white as sheep 's milk while others are as green as Persian vegetables. The riverbed here is paved with all kinds of stones with jade embedded among them." The Yulong River east of Hotan today was known in history as the White Jade River, where jade was finely ground with other minerals as a result of ages of erosion. The "white as sheep 's milk" quality was highly prized. These stones, in particular, were ideal for the carving of figurines, birds, small animals, flowers, small plants and grass, and landscapes.

According to the Daoist principles of Chinese cosmology, it is said that jade, like the moon, was regarded to be an object of *yin*. Under moonlight, jade which lay in the river would reflect itself with silvery rays on the water 's surface.

There are also rivers in China which became famous because of the color of the jade they produced. There are white jade rivers, green jade rivers, and dark jade rivers. According to the *History of the New Five Dynasties*, when autumn came and the river became low, it was the time to look for jade. Ordinary people, however, were not permitted to search for jade in a river if it had already come under the control of the local bureaucracy.

*Tales from the Western Regions* also contains vivid descriptions of collecting jade stones in Hotan during the Qing Dynasty: pebbles of varying sizes paving the flat riverbed were dotted with small jade stones. The jade collecting process was conducted under the strict control of officials. Away in the distance on the bank, a guard stood watch. On the bank near the water, was another guard. Skilled laborers hand-picked by the local government because of their reliability spread out in a line perpendicular to the river's flow. There would be twenty or thirty, depending on the width of the river. They waded in the water abreast, carefully feeling with their feet, employing their experience. Once they found a piece of jade, they bent down to pick it up and the workers on the bank could beat the gong once. Other officials would immediately record the finding with a red mark on paper to ensure that the number of jade stones found from the river would tally accurately.

As Hotan jade was rare, the Qing government enforced strict measures to ensure a total monopoly of the extremely valuable stone. In a report prepared in the autumn of 1807, officials not only kept accurate figures of the jade stones found from Hotan and its neighboring areas, but also classified them by weight and color. The report kept clear records of how many pieces, each piece's weight and color— up to ten different shades—and where in the river they were found.

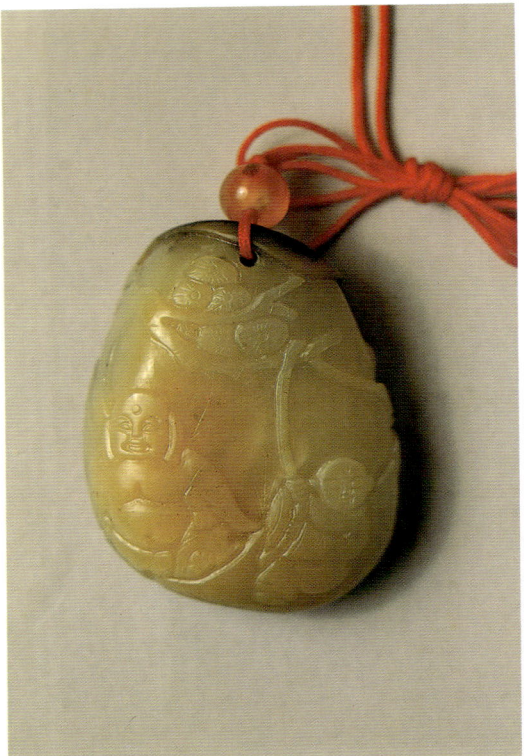

Jade pendant with figure
design (contemporary)

## 2. Defining Jade Quality

𝓑ecause the physical properties of jade are so varied, and are subject to a wide range of artistic interpretations, it is difficult to give
blanket appraisals as to jade quality in specific terms.

Overall, however, natural stones which have a fair finish with
elegant colors and whose chemical processes are stable can all be cat-
egorized as jade. There are two distinct categories: soft and hard. Soft
jades refer to calamite—jade formed by stralite minerals, including
white, green and yellow jade. Hard jades are green jade whose shapes

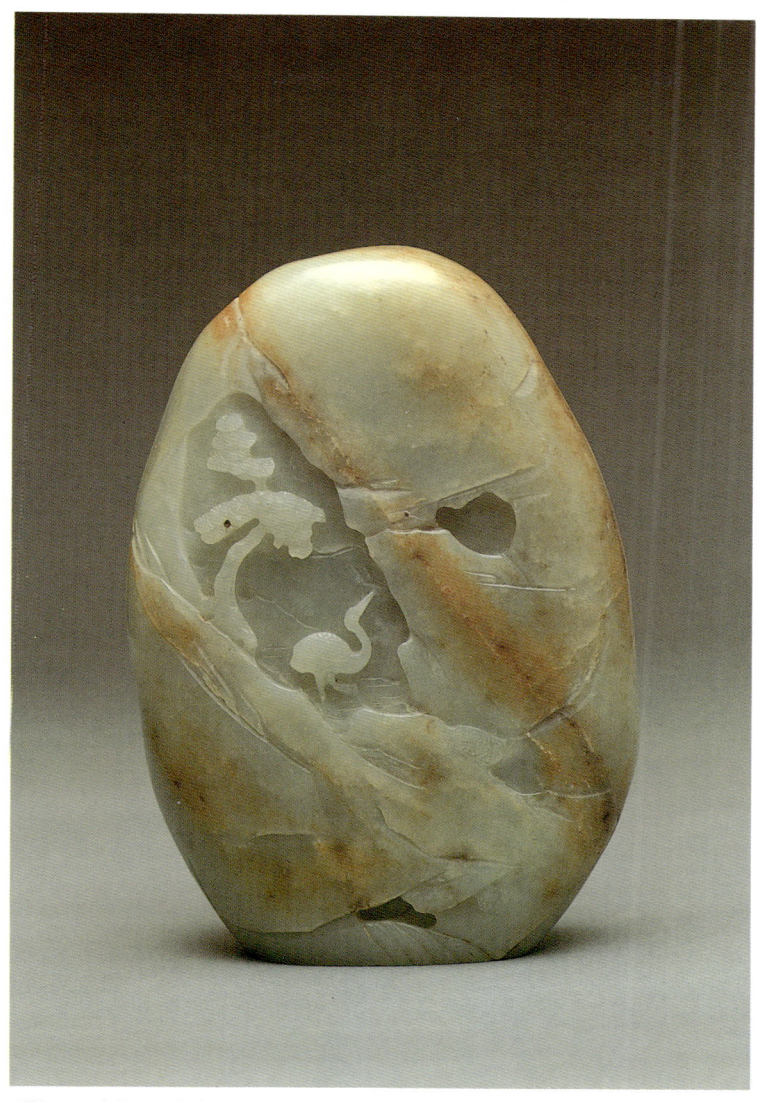

"Pine and Crane," decorative jade object (Qing Dynasty)

8

are similar to soft jade. The requirements for both hard and soft jade tend to be more or less the same, i.e., the molecular structure must be solid and the color must be naturally shiny and bright. White jade and green jade are normally considered gemstones regardless of their hard or soft attributes.

Emperor Taizong (r. 627-649) of the Tang Dynasty once remarked: "Though a jade stone may have high quality as a kind of stone, it is no more valuable than a piece of broken brick without the sophisticated work by craftsmen." The level of craftsmanship in carving jade, therefore, is an important factor when assessing the value of a piece of jade. It must possess an elegant and harmonious design, demonstrate a sophisticated carving technique, and project a refined and smooth finish. Other factors such as the period in which the object was made, the historical significance, or the social position of the owners, and the unique shapes and characteristics of the object itself all have an influence on value.

An archaeologist may normally look at the jade object with a different eye. Apart from the abovementioned factors, he may be overjoyed in seeing a broken and rather unattractive looking piece of jade. The reason? The piece of jade may help solve a major mystery in an archaeological puzzle.

The discovery of the Liangzhu jade pendant is a case in point. Used by the Liangzhu culture more than 4,000 years ago, such pendants have squared edges surrounding a round hole in the middle. Comprising several sections, they are decorated with carved figures and animal patterns. Many such pieces have been passed down through the generations among collectors both in and outside China. Until the 1970s, Liangzhu pieces were often mistaken for Han Dynasty (206 BC-AD 220) objects.

In 1972, an archaeological team unearthed a jade pendant along with pottery artifacts that had already been generally ascertained by scholars as belonging to the Liangzhu Culture. The location of the discovery was a tomb at Caoxie in Wuxian County, Jiangsu Province. It was then that this pendant was known to have originated far earlier than originally thought.

Jade pendant (contemporary)

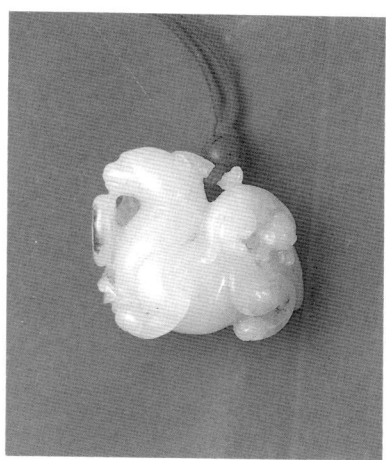

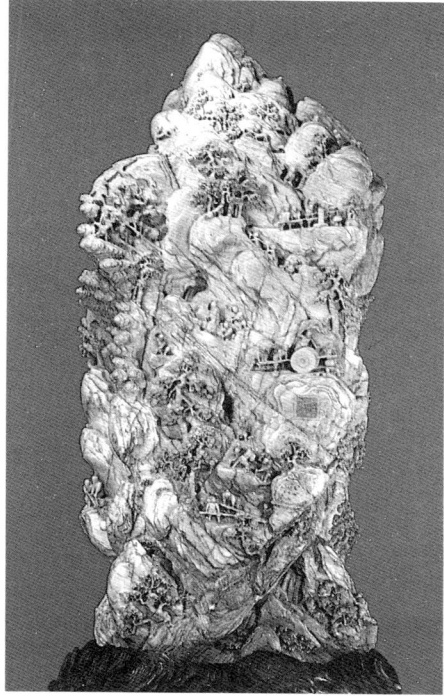

"Great Yu Taming the Flood," a carving on a single block of jade (Qing Dynasty)

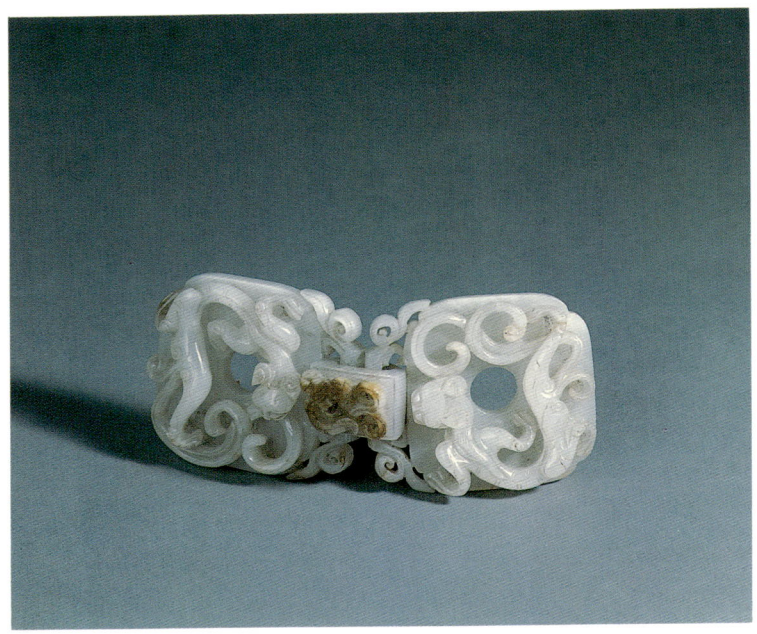

White jade belt buckle with double-dragon design (Yuan Dynasty)

White jade Qilin (Kirin),
a legendary Chinese
animal (Qing Dynasty)

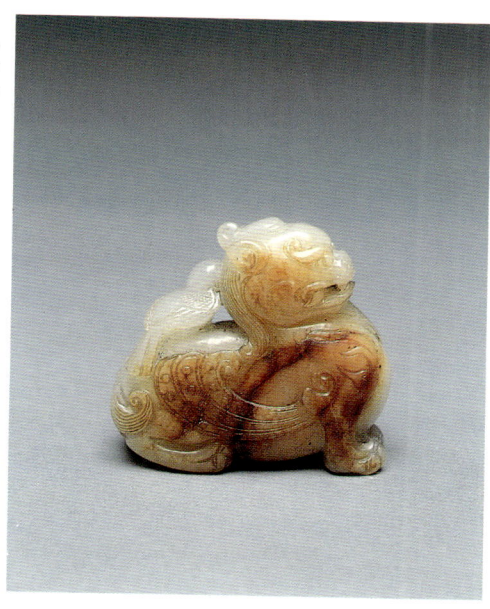

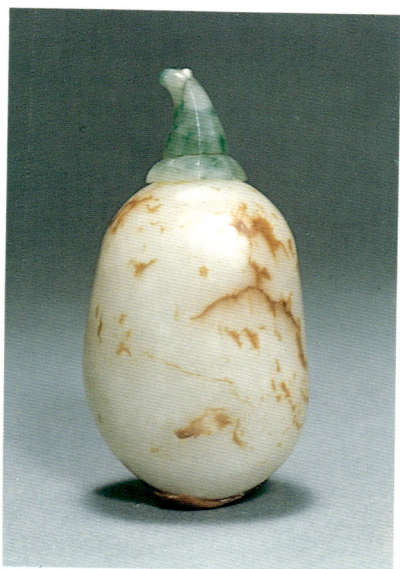

Melon-shaped white jade
pot with jadeite cover
(Qing Dynasty)

### 3. Symbols of Good Fortune

$\mathcal{P}$eople often encounter many jade objects which are carved in the shape of bats or gourds. In facts, themes of jade carving in China cover virtually every animate and inanimate object known, including legendary figures, birds, animals, stars, clouds, mountains, rivers, trees, grass and flowers.

The emergence of bats and gourds as subjects of jade carving was a phenomenon which appeared later in history. In the case of bats, or *bian fu*, the second character (*fu*) is synonymous with the Chinese word for wealth.

The Chinese name for gourd (*hu lu*) also sounds very similar to the Chinese word for wealth, and thus became a natural theme of jade carving. Such tradition reached its height during the Ming (1368-1644) and Qing (1644-1911) dynasties.

In jade carving, the image of the bat is often combined with other elements such as peaches (symbols of longevity), magpies (symbolizing happiness), lotus plants (representing harmony), and lotus seeds (representing fertility) to create images of happiness, good fortune, a large family, and a long life.

A rooster and a cockscomb flower presented together in a piece of jade carving carry the connotation of "official on top of another official," as the Chinese word for the crest of the rooster and the name of the flower both sound like the word for "official." Such work satisfied the desire of those people who wished to occupy high official positions. Works of this nature have embodied an aesthetic sensibility typical of Chinese society.

In artistic expressions, painters and sculptors are divided into realistic, abstract, and impressionist schools. In addition, there is the "wild animal school" which emphasizes an unbridled, wild and self-appreciative style of art. Superficially, Chinese jade carving technique belongs to the realistic school as its portrayal of flowers, birds, and figures are vividly visible. The truly deep meaning of the works, however, comes from the borrowing of names for the pronunciation of objects. Which school does such works belong to then? This technique is very similar to the practice of forbidding the use of certain words, a unique tradition deep-rooted in the Chinese culture at a very early time. According to this practice, words and their homonyms containing the names of emperors were forbidden to be used by the common people. Jade objects have always been symbols of the good and beautiful, while the practice of forbidding the use of certain words had always been associated with punishment.

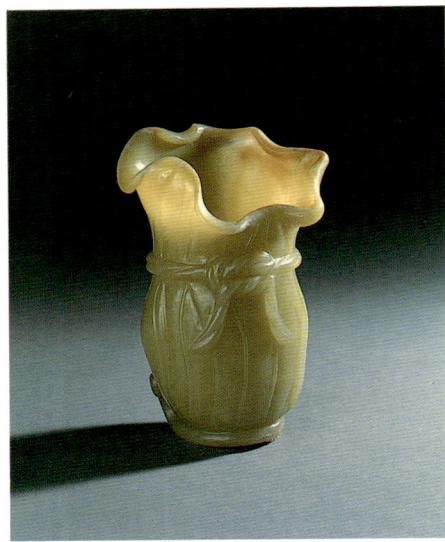

Topaz vase (Qing Dynasty)

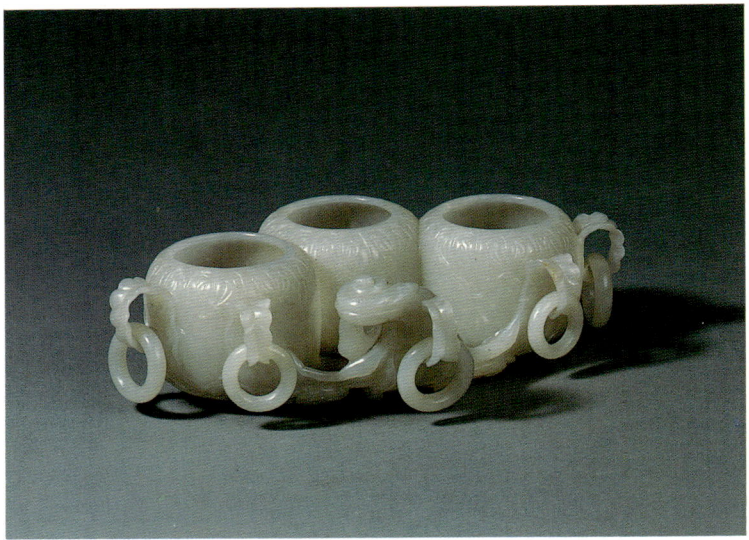

Three interconnecting sapphire jade cups (Qing Dynasty)

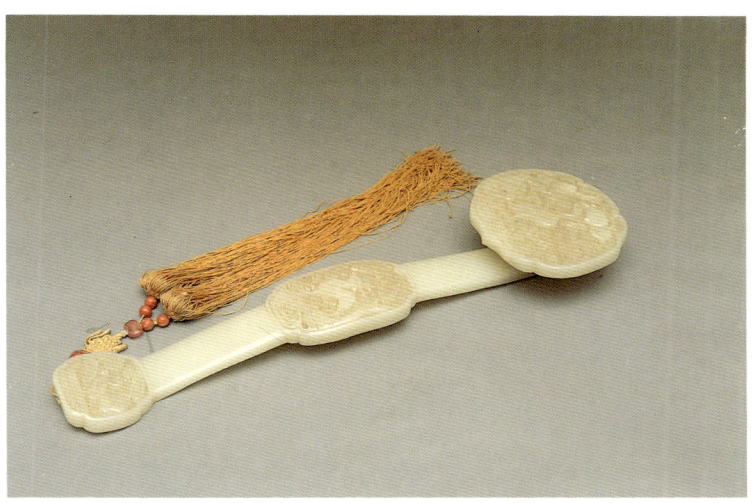

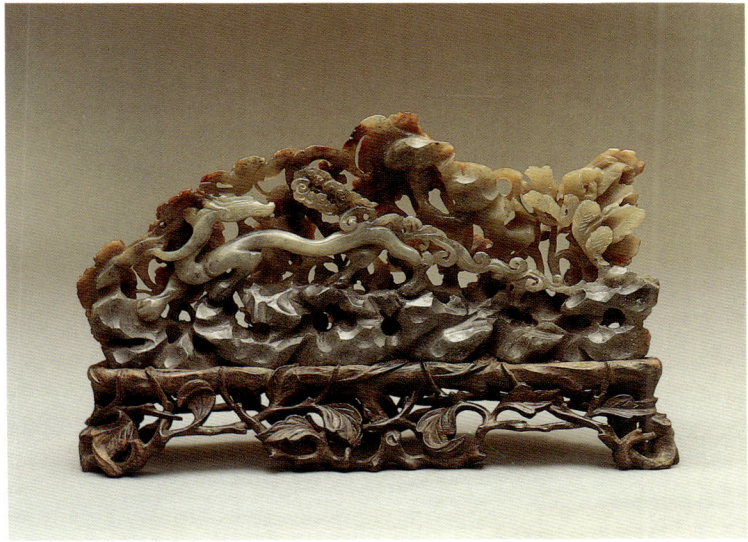

*Top:* White jade "Good Wishes" object (Qing Dynasty)
*Bottom:* Sapphire flowers and plants (Qing Dynasty)

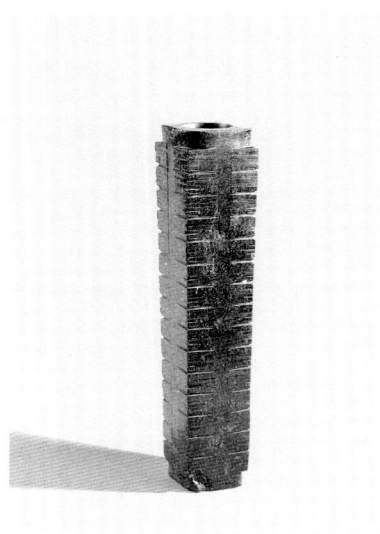

Multi-section jade object in square
shape with a hole in the middle
(Liangzhu Culture)

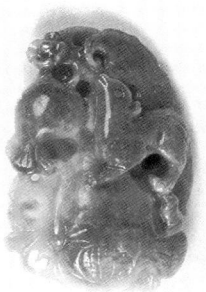

Jade pendant with animal and
fruit designs (contemporary)

## 4. The Emperor's Insatiable Appetite for Jade

*T*hroughout history there have been many people who have been captivated by the brilliance and subtlety of jade. Bian He, the abovementioned man from the State of Chu, was the subject of a famous parable by causing himself trouble when presenting a piece of raw, unfinished jade to the king. Bian He loved jade to the degree of neglecting his own safety. King Zhao of the State of Qin, a very covetous man, was condemned for having traded control of fifteen towns for a piece of jade. By contrast, Emperor Qianlong of the Qing Dynasty (whose reign lasted from 1736 to 1795) was a jade lover who pursued his hobby in a healthy and constructive way.

Throughout history, Chinese emperors were almost always associated with their easy and elegant lifestyle, their pursuit of excess and debauchery, their large groups of concubines, and their seemingly endless streams of imperial edicts. On top of this, Emperor Qianlong was known throughout the empire for his grand tours to China's southern regions. Emperor Qianlong began to study literature at the age of nine. He learned archery and studied the techniques of warfare. After he ascended to the throne, he ordered the compilation of numerous books about art, including painting and calligraphy, bronzes, ancient coins, and other cultural treasures. What is most striking, however, is not how Qianlong busied himself with state affairs, but rather the degree to which he poured himself into the study, collection, and appreciation of jade.

Highly skilled at writing and composing prose, the emperor left behind no fewer than 800 separate writings about jade. Qianlong had attained an extremely advanced level as to his knowledge, appreciation, and assessment of jade, as well as the study of its historiography, past masters, and the advocating or promotion of certain styles.

Since modern-era field research concerning jade artifacts was begun rather late in China, most round, flat jade pieces with a hole in the middle were thought by archaeologists to date from the Han Dynasty.

Even during the reign of Emperor Qianlong, references to the study of these jade objects were scarce. In his early studies, the emperor was both influenced and restricted by the historical views of the time. As he gained experience in his careful examination of the jade pieces, he eventually concluded that they dated from a time earlier than the Han Dynasty. In his writings he questioned many times

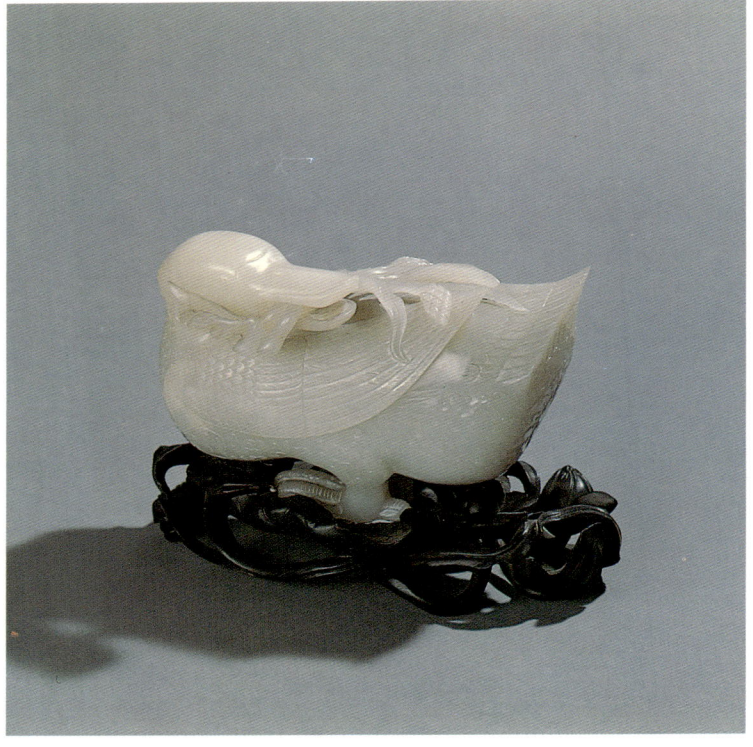

Sapphire duck (Qing Dynasty)

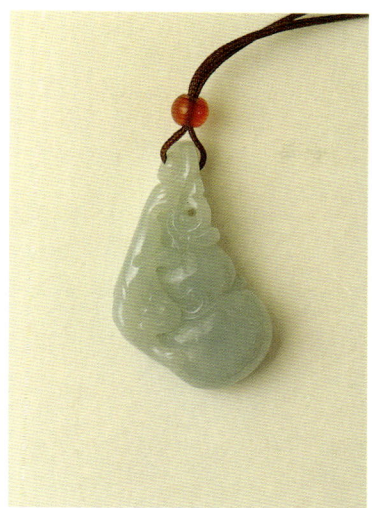
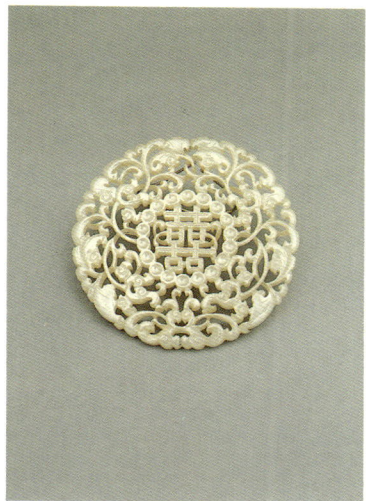
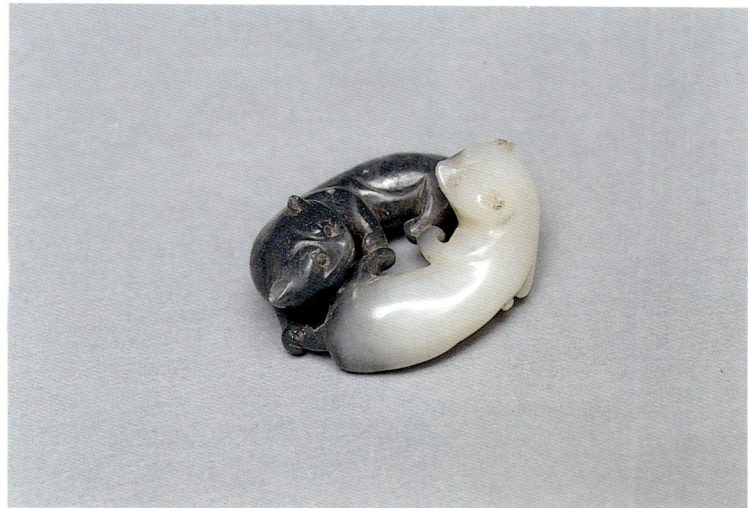

*Top left:* Gourd-shaped jadeite pendant (contemporary)
*Top right:* Double-happiness white jade plaque (Qing Dynasty)
*Bottom:* Jade pendant in the form of double badgers (Qing Dynasty)

how objects used during the Zhou Dynasty (c. 1100 BC-221 BC) are called Han Dynasty (206 BC-AD220) jades? As he continued his research, he later was able to date the objects to an even earlier time, a period before 2100 BC which was the last stage of prehistoric society in China. This find was surprisingly close to the period of more than 4,000 years ago, a date generally accepted among archaeologists today.

Emperor Qianlong found that several jade cups in the palace contained a layer of brown glaze of different shades as if the color had been applied to the cups. When he rubbed the cups, the layer of brown glaze seemed to have not been submerged in the cup body. He initially concluded that they were from the Han Dynasty, but when he had proof against this method of dating, he was at loss as to exactly when the cups were made.

He then unexpectedly went to consult a jade sculptor, Yao Zongren, from Suzhou, who often created work in the style of ancient objects. Yao admitted that the cups had been produced by his ancestors, saying that they had all lived by imitating ancient works. Listening attentively, the emperor asked him many other questions. Yao then told the emperor every technique that had been handed down in his family through the generations. The emperor, who found Ya o 's explanations enlightening, told the artisan what had led him to question the authenticity of the cups and concluded that they were not originals from the Han Dynasty. Then he recorded his conversation with Mr. Yao and attached a piece of .the written record to each of the three cups. The three cups, have been preserved to this day, which, still stay together with the record written by the emperor.

The emperor was also learned in the methods of processing jade as well as various styles and techniques of jade carving. He strongly advocated rendering the carvings with a landscape painting-like quality and shaped them according to the specific qualities and attributes of the natural jade. Beginning from the 25th year of his reign, the hinterland region of Xinjiang offered 2,000 kilograms of jade to the royal court as tribute which greatly enhanced the development of the craft of jade carving.

However, a trend soon emerged which began to emphasize

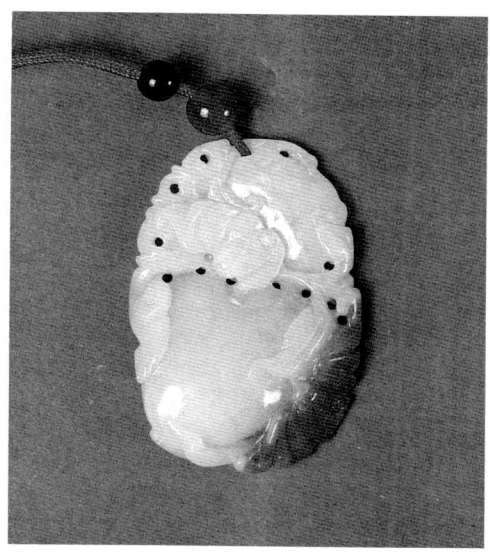

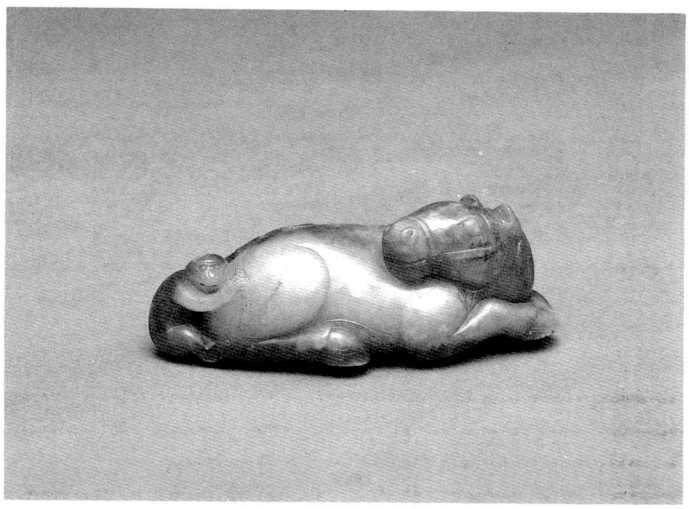

*Top:* Jadeite pendant with the theme of longevity (contemporary)
*Bottom:* Sapphire carving of a horse with a monkey, symbol for nobility (Qing Dynasty)

quantity rather than quality in the production of arts and handicrafts for general consumption. Artisans showed a restless state of mind and pursued a clever yet fancy style, a development strongly condemned by the emperor on several occasions. Qianlong even went to such an extent as to ordering the removal of ropes added to a jade ox because he found them redundant. To reverse this undesirable trend in jade carving, the emperor advocated imitation of the ancient carving style. Interestingly he even told artisans to carve false accreditations and then bake the objects so as to make them look like originals

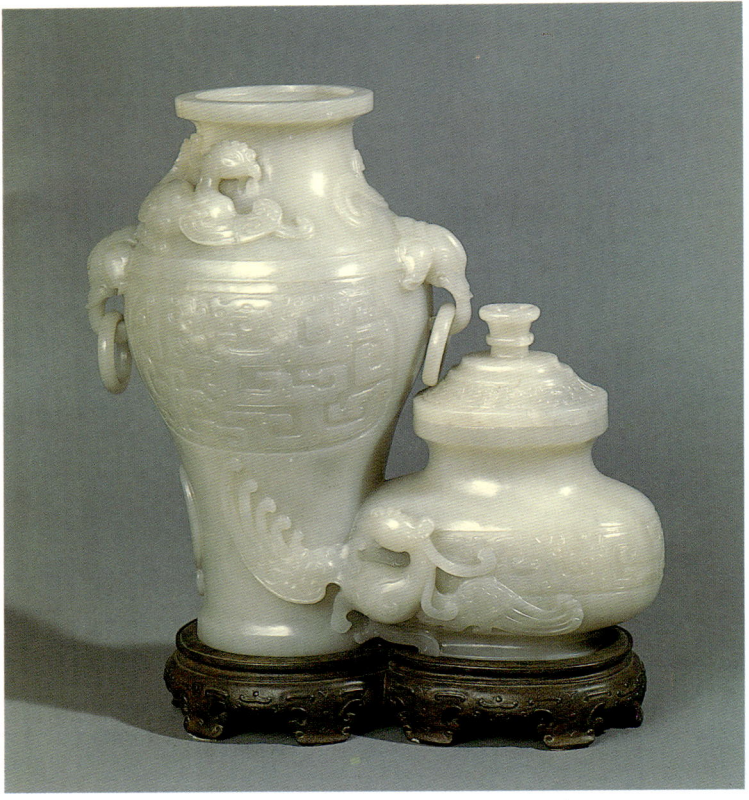

Connected sapphire vases (Qianlong period, Qing Dynasty)

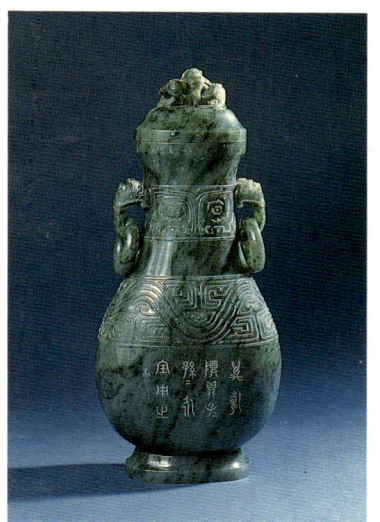

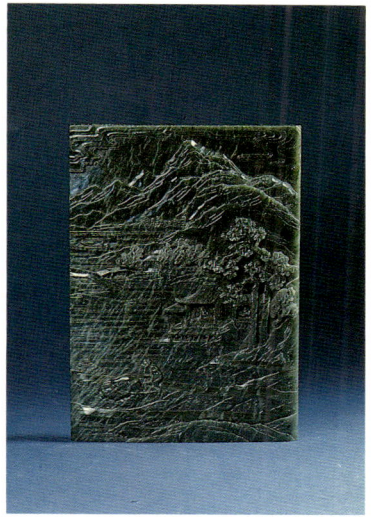

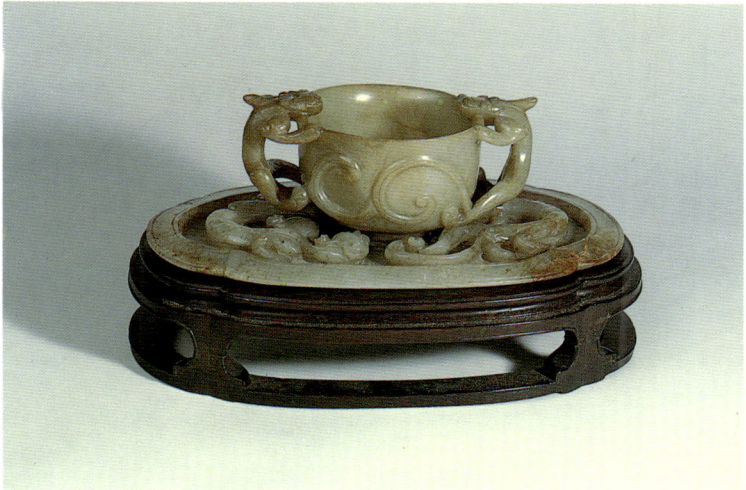

*Top left:* Jasper covered vase with animal mask design (Qianlong period, Qing Dynasty)

*Top right:* Jasper table screen with the theme of farming and reading (Qianlong period, Qing Dynasty)

*Bottom:* Sapphire bowl with double dragon designs (Qianlong period of the Qing Dynasty)

of ancient times. Thus, it was the emperor himself who became the man behind the production of imitation jades in the palace workshop. What is especially intolerable to later generations was that the emperor, a devotee of jade, even had his own inscriptions carved on original jade objects of earlier times, turning objects of true art into political and social statements reflecting the times.

## 5. Legends of Ancient Jade Objects

*I*n the book, *A Detailed Account of Ancient Jade Ware*, Xu Zhenglun wrote: "If you understand ancient jade, you will understand the Chinese people and their culture, because the culture of ancient jade is the culture of China. Stories of the jade culture are exactly stories of the more than a billion Chinese." Jade culture is indeed a critical part of the deep-rooted tradition and culture of China. Jade culture has existed throughout the history of China and embodies many colorful, mysterious, and interesting tales.

Xu Chu of the Han Dynasty once made the remark that "Jade crystallizes the beauty of stones." He personified jade as having "five great virtues," namely, righteousness, benevolence, intelligence, gallantry, and uprightness. Other ancient books listed nine and even ten virtues of jade. It is perhaps a unique characteristic of Chinese culture to compare the qualities of jade with those of human beings.

There are more than 500 Chinese characters with the word of jade as particles and people love to use the word of jade to describe good things and objects. For example, a "jade girl" simply means a beautiful young girl. A "jade hand" means a very dexterous, slender, and attractive hand. The term "jade picture" is always used to refer to a well-taken portrait photograph. Even in describing somebody who becomes a martyr for a good cause, he or she does not die but rather the "jade has fallen into pieces." Literary and biographical writings are not short of emotional tales about jade and its relationship to society.

"A Handful of Snow" was originally a name coined for an extremely valuable jade cup. Li Yu of the early Qing Dynasty even created a well known scripted drama based on this legendary jade cup. Two of the main characters, Mo Huaigu and Tang Qin, were old friends. In order to win the favor of Yan Shifan, a man of influence and wealth, Tang framed his old friend Mo and took away "A Handful of Snow" which he presented to the despotic Yan. Mo's loyal

26

servant sacrificed himself to save the life of his master while Mo's concubine managed to kill the traitor Tang and then committed suicide. In the end, Yan fell from grace and the cup was returned to the hand of Mo's son. Furthermore, Mo and his wife finally were reunited with each other. This tale has become a favorite theme for several Peking operas on modern and contemporary theatrical stages.

Another story mentioned previously called "The Jade Pendant" is about a man named Bian He who found a piece of uncut jade on a mountain. Out of loyalty to the sovereign ruler, he presented the raw

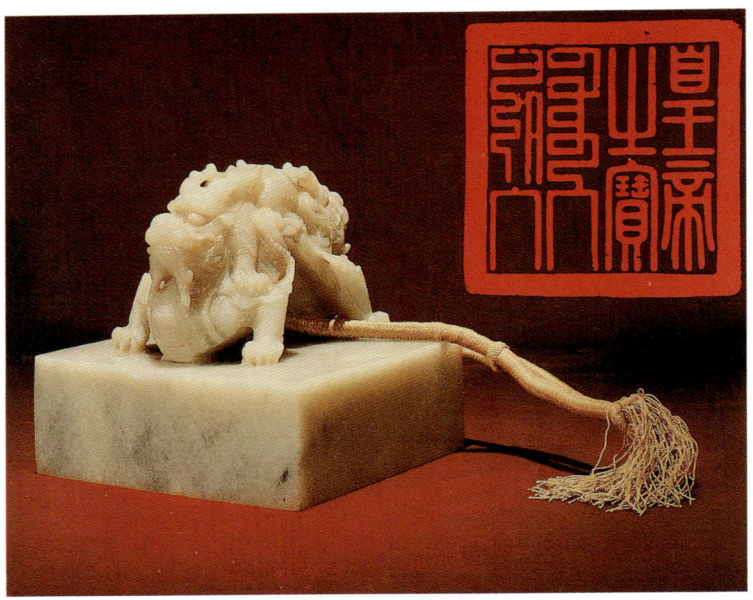

Imperial jade seal (Qing Dynasty)

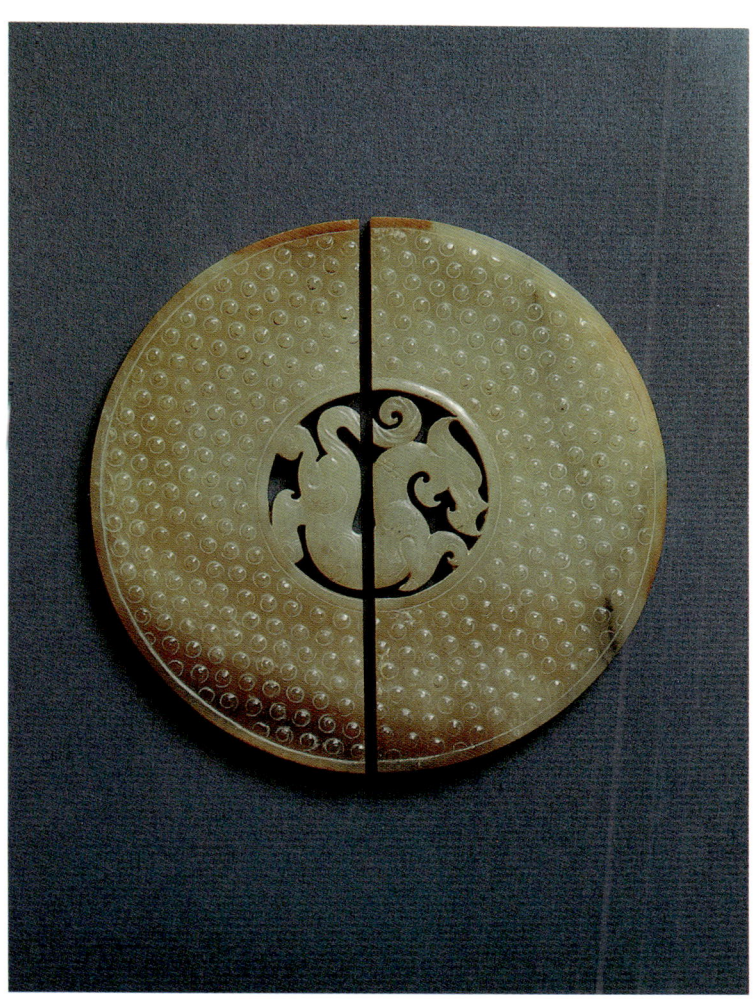

Sapphire disc with openwork carving of a dragon (Warring States Period)

jade to King Li and later King Wu of the State of Chu, only to be punished by having both feet cut off by the kings who did not recognize the value of the stone, thinking it merely some worthless rock. When King Wen took the throne, Bian He wanted to offer his jade to the new king. By that time he was already well advanced in age and could not walk, no longer having his feet. In despair, he cried for three days on the mountain, holding his piece of uncut jade. When he had no more tears, blood came out of his eyes. This moved the new king who ordered artisans to carve the jade into a pendant based on its natural shape. The new king then rewarded Bian He by naming the work: "He's Jade Pendant."

Perhaps because the quality of He's jade pendant was unusually good, the craftsmanship superior, and the type of raw jade itself was rare, events soon unfolded which would focus on this particular piece of jade.

To fulfill his wish of taking possession of the jade pendant, King Zhao of Qin (r. 295-251 BC) used a ruse by presenting fifteen towns to the State of Zhao in exchange for the jade. The king of the State of Zhao had to send his prime minister as an envoy to the State of Qin. The prime minister turned out to be an exceptionally clever man who managed to have the jade pendant returned to his home state. The quietness over the state of affairs concerning the jade, however, did not last long. In 228 BC, the Qin army rolled into the State of Zhao, annexing it—and the famous jade pendant in the process. Since then, the whereabouts of the pendant became a mystery. A generally accepted story is recorded in the famous historical classic written by Sima Qian, entitled *Records of the Historian*, which was written during the Han Dynasty. The book quoted Cui Hao as saying that He's jade pendant was kept at the Han court for more than 200 years, cherished by each Han emperor as a national treasure. By the Tang Dynasty, it had resurfaced, only to be destroyed in 936 AD when the last emperor of the Tang Dynasty burned himself to death at Xuanwu Tower, along with the jade pendant.

*Chinese Tales: Past and Present* also records that a man named Sun Wentai had gotten hold of a saddle carved from sapphire, which supposedly had such brilliance it was found to be able to illuminate a road at night.

The official seal of the First Emperor of Qin was said to have been adapted from He's jade pendant, and it too could illuminate. When Sun Jian stationed his troops south of the city of Luoyang, then occupied by Dong Zhuo, Sun saw colorful beams sparkling out from a nearby well. He ordered workers into the well and there they found the First Empero r's official seal. The square seal, about 1.5 inches each side, was carved with five dragons on the handle. One corner of the seal was damaged but it revealed characters in the handwriting of Li Si, prime minister under the First Emperor of Qin, announcing the mandate of heaven, the divine rule by which the emperor had the right to govern.

Du Guangting, a Taoist master active toward the last years of the Tang Dynasty (618-907), wrote that He's jade pendant, before it was adapted into the empero r's official seal, could indeed change color and project illumination, sending out different colors under different lighting conditions. Modern scientists believe that such jade was most likely composed of fluorite with phosphorescent qualities or made of pink ice crystals.

Toward the end of the Qing Dynasty, Wu Lan wrote another preface for Chen Xing's *A Chronology of Jade*, in which he discussed his surprise meeting with one of his relative named Du Xiaofang in Hubei. Du showed him an ancient jade bracelet, saying that whenever a change in the weather was to take place, misty, white moisture would appear on the bracelet. Wu tested it several times, which all proved his relative 's statement to be true.

There is another story according to which that when thieves were trying to steal burial objects by digging open an ancient tomb during the reign of Emperor Jing of Wu, they found in the coffin a corpse whose body color was like that of a living person. People explained that this was the result of placing several dozen pieces of white jade next to the body in the coffin. A Chinese medicinal classic recorded that if someone swallowed 3 lbs of jade before death, for three years after his death, his body would not change color.

*The Book of Strange Tales* says that in the ancient Baishi Kingdom, every resident had a complexion as white as jade. They did not culti-

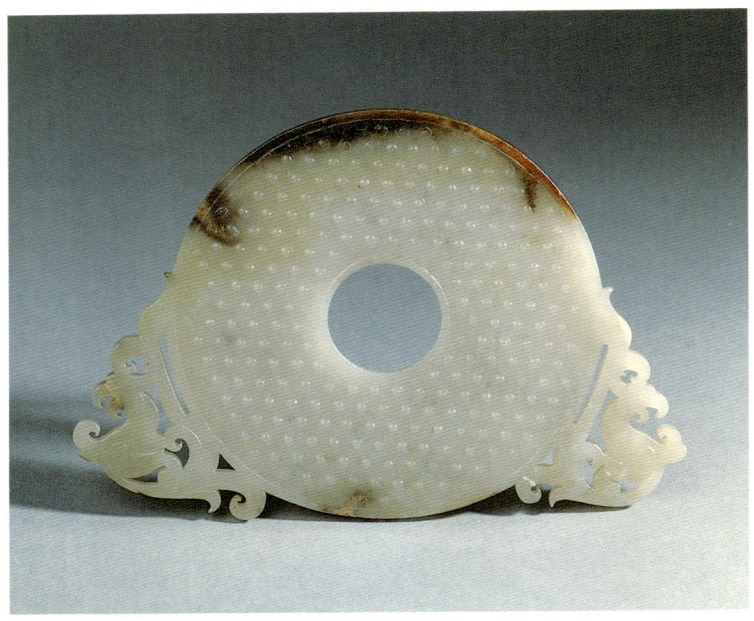

White jade disc with double-phoenix design (Warring States Period)

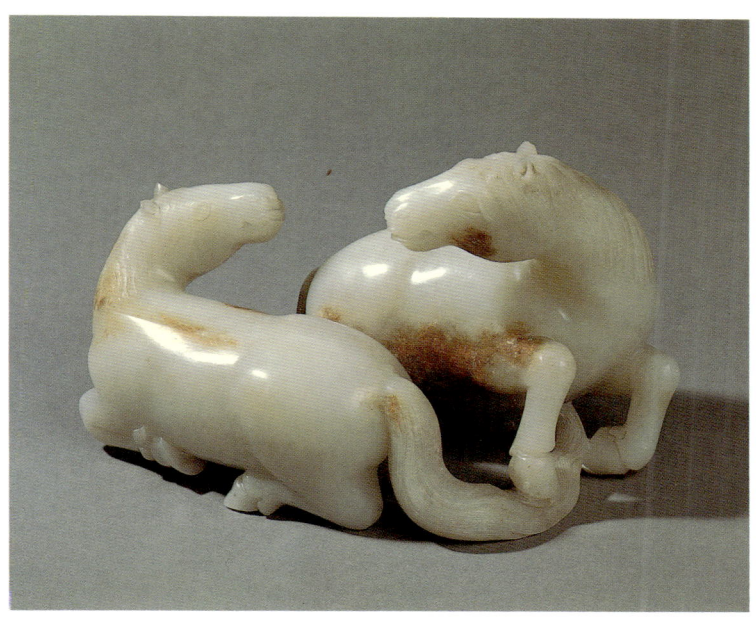

Sapphire horses (Qing Dynasty)

vate grain crops but planted jade instead. They would grind jade into powder which was both nourishing and delicious. When they entertained guests, they treated them to wine sprinkled with jade powder. One Chinese gallon of the wine could keep someone intoxicated for three years. Thus people in the kingdom were all said to live beyond 1,000 years!

Another book tells the story about Feng Yuehua, beloved concubine of Shen Xiaozhi, a governor of Jingzhou during the Song Dynasty (581-618). The lady had a jade horse with a green rein. She would take off the rein and put the horse and rein next to her pillow before she went to bed. They would immediately turn into a white horse with green reins in the horse shed. Before daybreak, they would return to their original shape. She examined the hooves of the jade horse and found dust underneath.

According to *The Ages of Kings and Emperors*, Empress Zhao of Han once saw a jade chicken with a red pearl in the mouth and immediately remarked that whoever swallowed the jade would be a king. She gulped down the jade soon gave birth to a boy who later became the founding emperor of the powerful Han Dynasty.

Interesting and strange stories about ancient Chinese jade are simply too numerous to repeat. Though many stories carry an obvious superstitious quality because of the time they were created, they nevertheless tell of the deep love, appreciation, dedication, and fascination for jade by the Chinese people.

## 6. Traditions and Treasures

*T*he culture of jade is not unique to China, however, because of the length of the historical record, jade and China are often mentioned in the same breath. It is the depth and breadth of history which makes the relationship so significant.

The earliest jade artifact found in China is believed to be the snake-like carvings unearthed from the Immortal's Cave, Haicheng, in Liaoning Province. The pieces date from 12,000 years ago. This discovery was followed by small decorative jade pieces such as the jade tablet in the form of a semi-circle and a jade ring from which a segment had been cut, uncovered from the ruins of the Hemudu Culture in modern day Zhejiang Province, which date from approximately 7,000 years ago. A jade earring and fragments of a larger jade ring have also been found in the lower levels of the ruins of the Majiabang Culture at Songze near Shanghai, which date to approximately 6,000 years ago. Within a different level of the same tomb were found a piece of jade placed in the mouth of the deceased, a jade tablet in the form of a semi-circle, and a jade ring which dated back more than 5,000 years. While somewhat abundant, jade objects of this period were largely unrefined due to the relatively primitive level of stone working implements. With the discovery of various methods and techniques of carving and grinding, the opportunity arose to create highly refined pieces of jade art.

Approximately 4,000 years ago, a great turning point in the history of Chinese civilization was reached. The Hongshan culture in the northeast and the Liangzhu culture in the region of Lake Tai in China's eastern area were noted for their advanced productivity and advanced social structure. Primitive forms of written Chinese characters appeared. The scale of development by which jade objects were used for ceremonial purposes represented the high level of co-development of the ritual systems, and heralded the first great period of jade use in Chinese history.

Another example of Hongshan culture was in the form of a green jade dragon 10 inches high, a Y-shaped jade mask bearing the design of an animal face, a hook-shaped jade pendant, and a jade ring. These treasures were unearthed in Sanxingtala Village of the Ongniud Banner region in Inner Mongolia. From the Liangzhu culture, examples of jade work included a jade square with a hole in the middle carved with thin lines of animal and human designs, 3.3 inches high and weighing 14 lbs; a long jade square with human face design and several knots 19.5 inches high. This piece is now kept at the British Museum; a ceremonial jade dagger with human and animal designs, and a jade bracelet carved with bird designs. The remarkable development of jade objects of this time reflected the extent to which

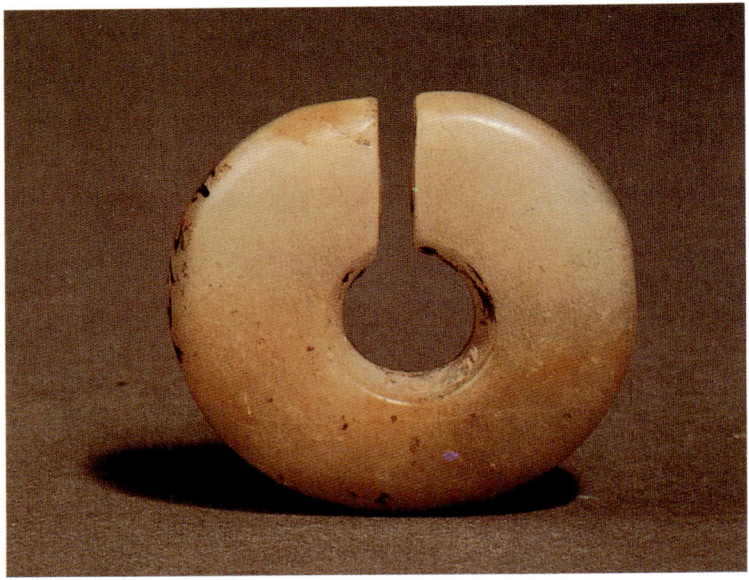

Jade ring with a segment cut off (Majiabang Culture)

Jade tablets in the form of a
semi-circle or near semi-circle
and jade rings with a segment
cut off (Hemudu Culture)

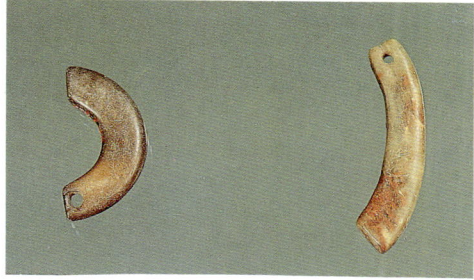

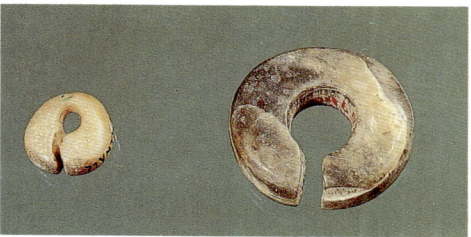

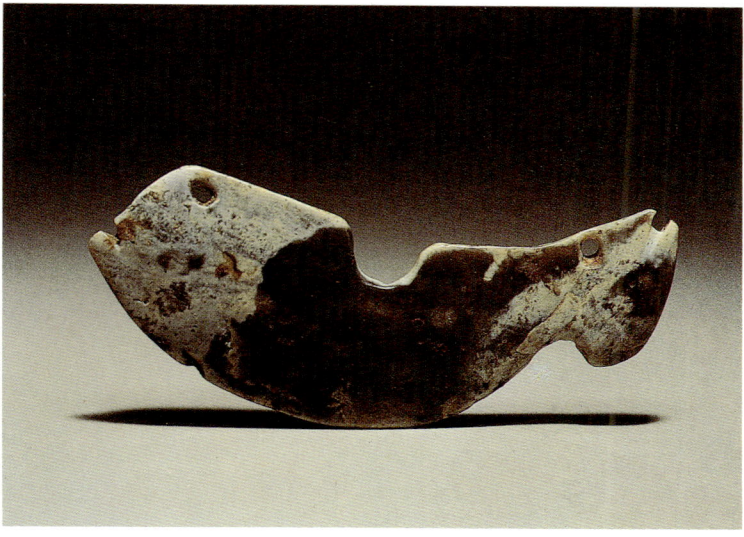

A jade tablet in the form of an animal (Songze Culture)

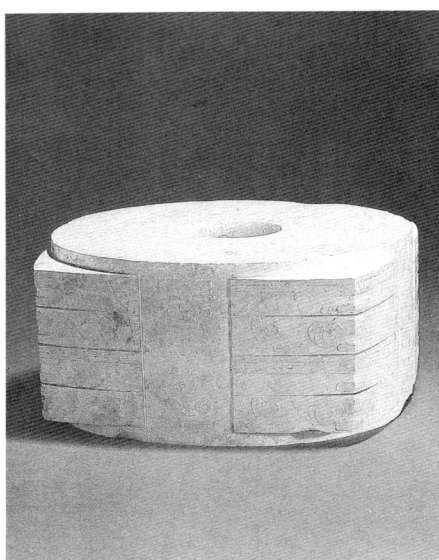

Hollow piece of jade with
animal and human designs
(Liangzhu Culture)

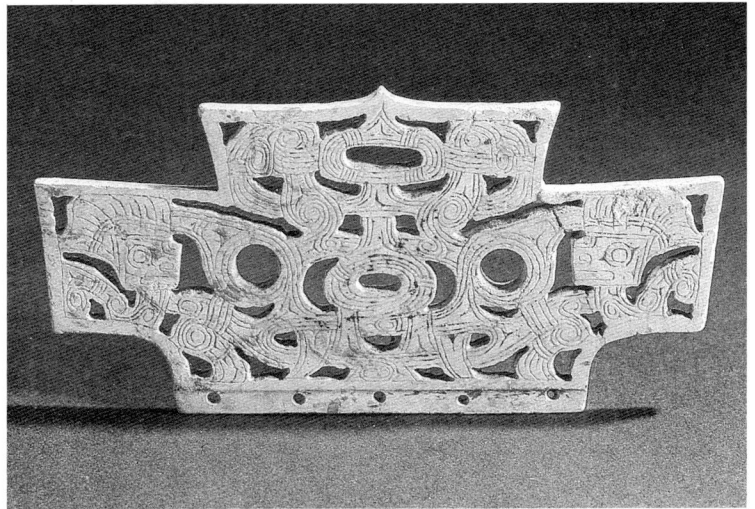

Jade with openwork animal and human designs (Liangzhu Culture)

A jade ring with a segment cut off in the shape of an animal (Hongshan Culture)

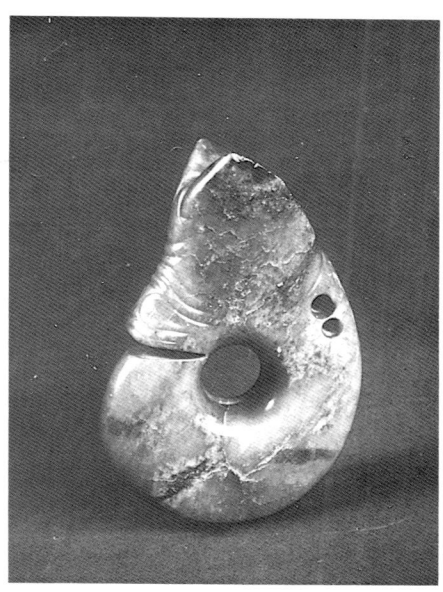

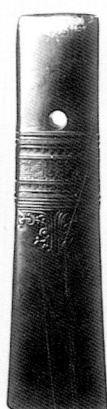

Jade object of the Longshan Culture

38

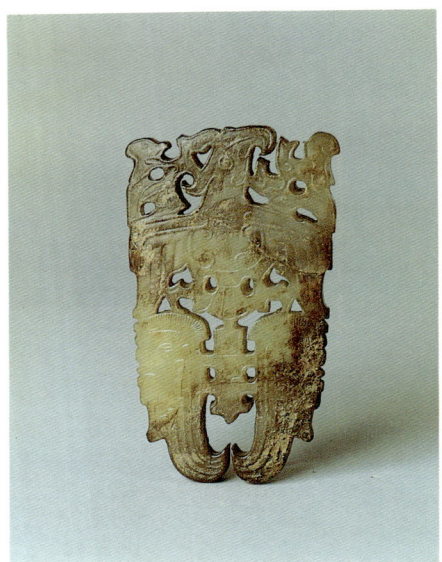

Sapphire with human mask design (Shang Dynasty)

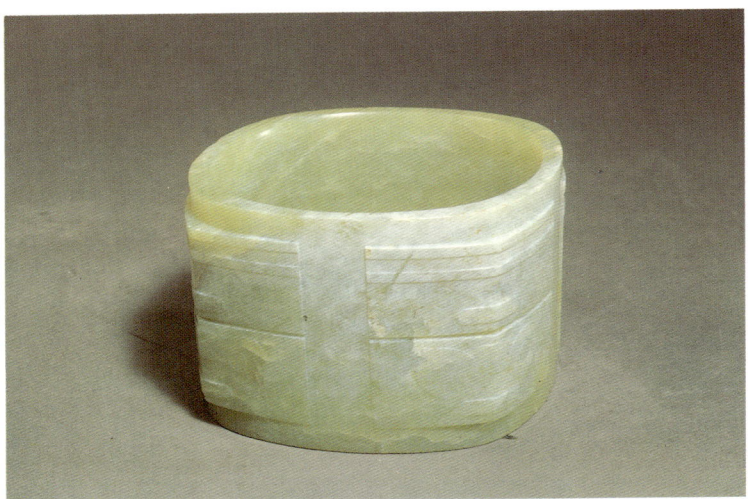

Jade bracelet with animal and human designs (Liangzhu Culture)

Jade figure (Shang Dynasty)

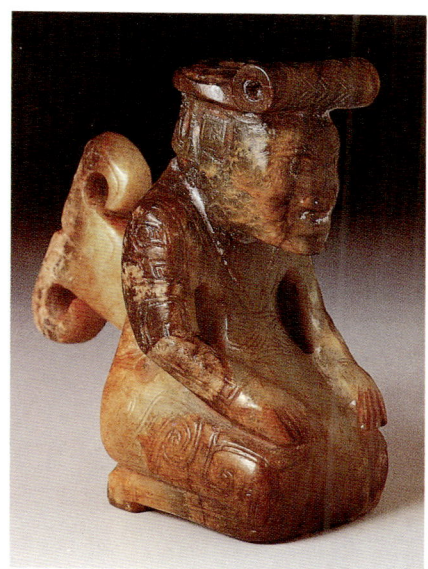

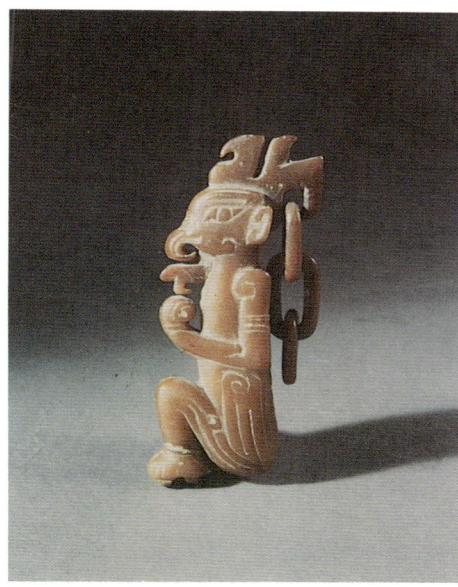

Bird-shaped jade figure
(Shang Dynasty)

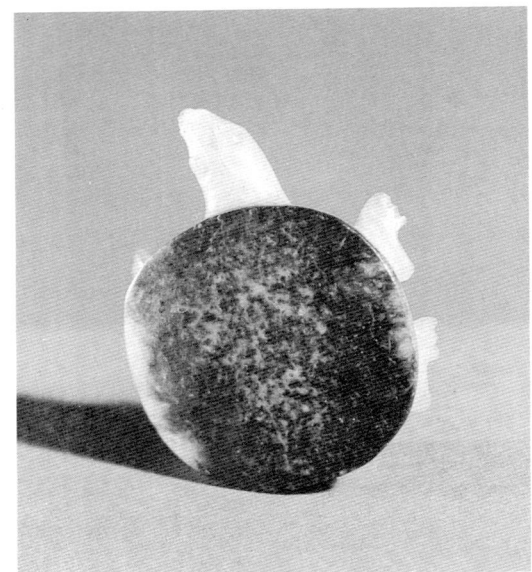

Two-color jade turtle
(Shang Dynasty)

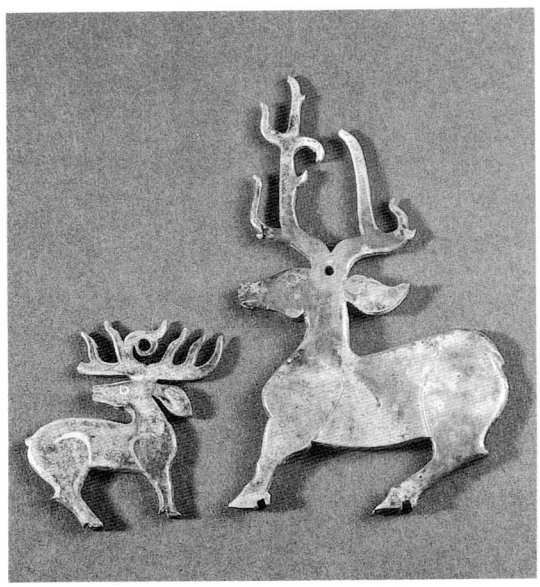

Jade deer (Zhou
Dynasty)

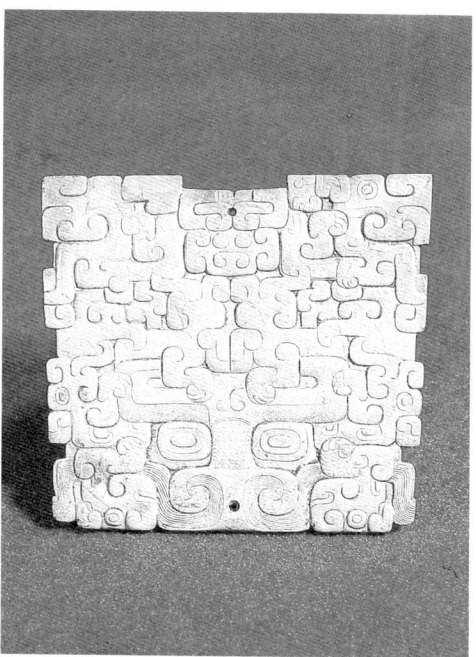

Jade plaque with animal
mask design (Spring &
Autumn Period)

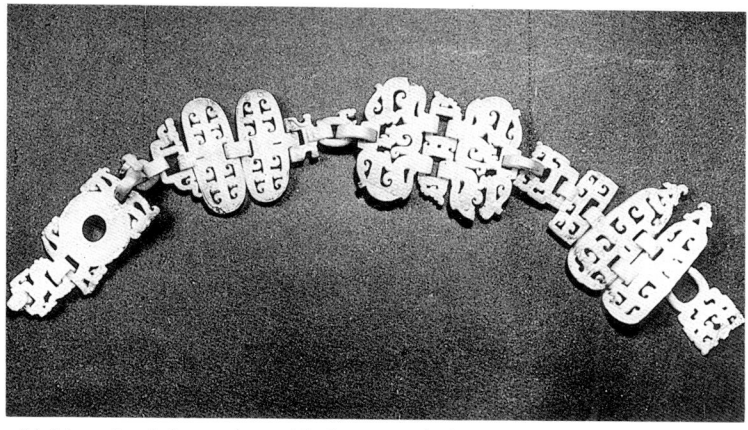

Multi-section jade pendant with dragon and phoenix designs (Warring
States Period)

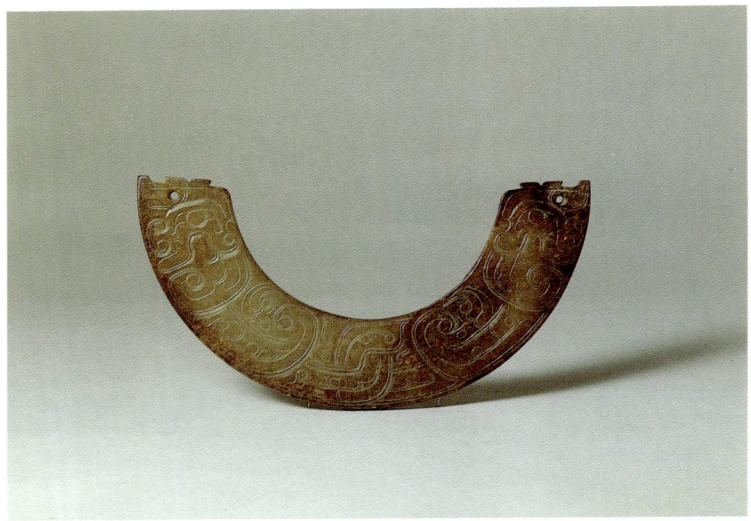

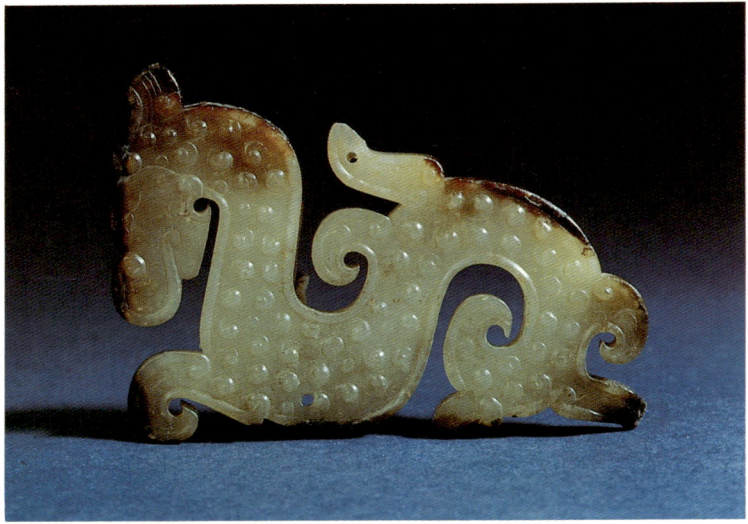

*Top:* Sapphire tablet with dragon design (Western Zhou)
*Bottom:* Sapphire dragon (Warring States Period)

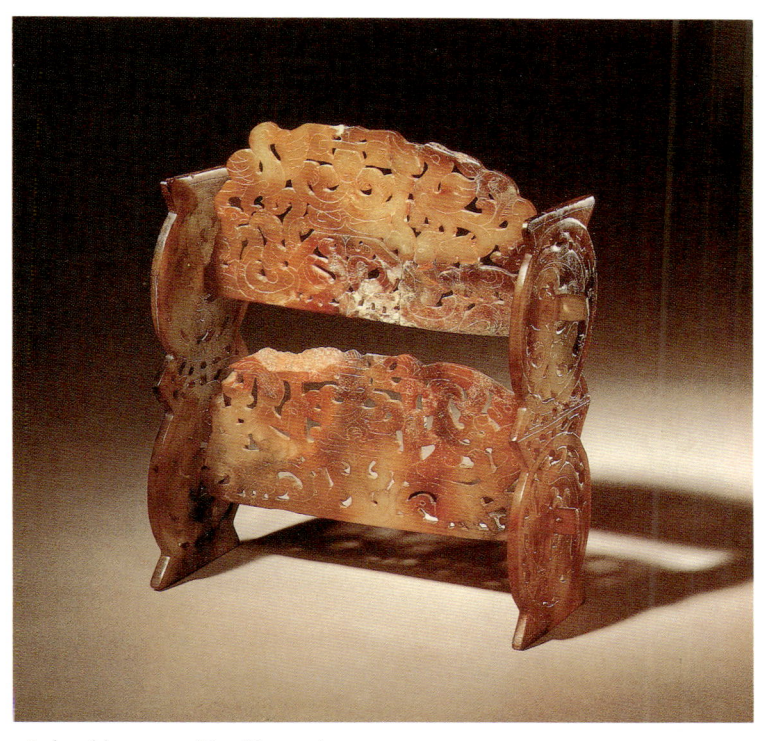

Jade table screen (Han Dynasty)

ancestor worship and divination influenced daily life. They also served to delineate the characteristics that were already prevalent during the Hongshan period, evolving into the elegant and refined characteristics typical of the Liangzhu Culture.

The Shang Dynasty (ca. 16th-11th centuries BC) marked the second peak period of jade use in Chinese history. The availability of Bronze Age metal tools brought the artistic design and carving techniques to a much higher level. Jade objects were carved into round shapes bearing geometrical pattern. The complexity of ritual activities increased the variety of jade objects used for ceremonial or funerary purposes. Swords, axes, halberds, and other items were representative works of this period. The nobility, perhaps envisioning turning into birds and flying to heaven after death, encouraged the creation of jade figures with bird decorations.

Jade objects of the later Western Zhou period showed still more variety, with pieces ranging from fish, birds and other animals. The most-often seen were jade swords or decorations featuring rough or intaglio lines cut on one side of the jade objects to portray bird or animal face designs.

The Spring and Autumn and the Warring States periods (ca 770-221 BC) was an era of great political division with many different schools of philosophical thought and art contending for influence upon the social landscape. Great improvements in the art of jade craft were observed. An artistic style with refined, compact, and rich layers of curving lines was typical of this period. The bodies of dragons and phoenixes decorating the animal-faced jade plaques rise and fall in a natural, flowing motion, creating a truly miraculous impression. The jade animal decorative objects unearthed from the tomb of Prince Jing of Zhongshan in Hebei Province, and the jade slab with curved edge found in Wuxian in Jiangsu Province, just to name two examples, were outstanding representative works of the period. Designs showing wood grain and even wooden nails were common on round-shaped pieces of jade with a hole in the middle, as well as S-shapes and various depictions of jade dragons. Refined lines were adopted to portray human hair and clothing. Metal inlaying techniques were often used as a way to restore "old" or "damaged" carved jade pieces. A 19-inch-long jade dragon pendant unearthed in Guwei Village, Huixian, Henan Province, was comprised of several sections, adapted from five pieces of old jade, totaling 26 sections and connected by eight rings. Dragon, phoenix and other animals were the dominant designs augmented with lines featuring silkworms, clouds, etc. Techniques such as cutting, flat carving, incised carving, removing the background; openwork cutting, drilling, and grinding were used. Such pieces are characteristic of jade art during the Spring and Autumn and Warring States periods.

The unification of China by the First Emperor of Qin and the prosperity attained during the subsequent Han Dynasty posed great challenges to the preexisting systems of ancestor worship, ritual, and divination. Jade craft, consequently, entered a new phase free from traditional ritual object manufacture. A wide range of objects, many of which were so abstract in shape that they had no practical values, including jade squares with a hole in the middle or jade pieces with a pointed tip, soon disappeared completely. Relief carving, round sculpture, and a much simpler, more concise methods of carving techniques soon became commonplace. The demand for art objects, decorations, or common items, together with the use of jade burial items increased in quantity.

The historical period covering the era of the Three Kingdoms, the Western Jin, Eastern Jin and the Northern and Southern Dynasties, from 220 to 589 AD, saw political turmoil and sporadic warfare in a struggle for conquest, political influence, and territory. The Chinese economy crumbled while jade lost its popularity.

By contrast, the Sui and Tang dynasties saw yet another period of great prosperity and unification. Art and culture flourished. Gold and silver, in particular, were among the fine metals used by artisans. Jade making should have made great headway in this regard, but great works from this period are surprisingly rare, with the exception of various decorative pieces with meticulously carved lions and other animal designs as well as floral patterns.

After the cultural heights reached during the Tang, the period of the Song, Liao, Kin and Yuan dynasties, extending from 960 to 1368, featured the continuation of low relief, high relief, and round sculp-

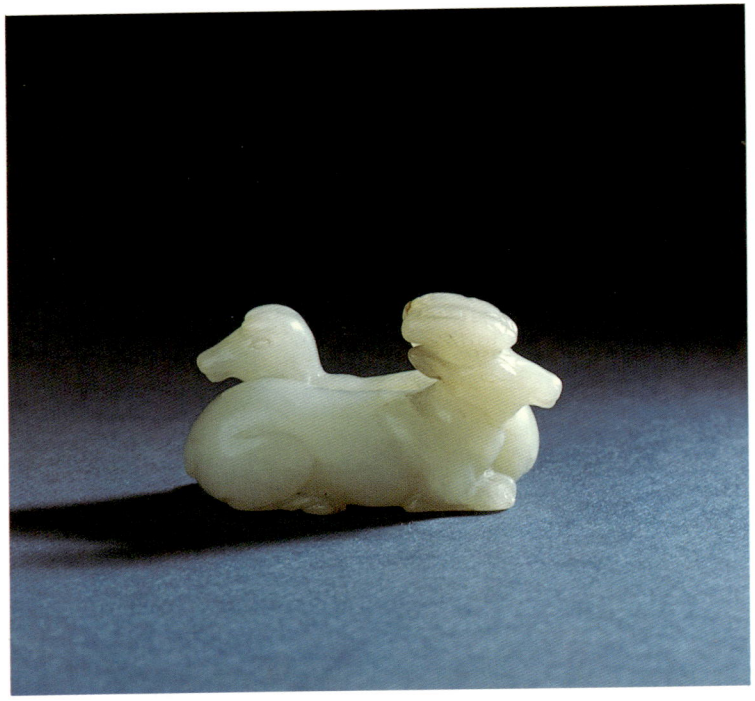

Sapphire pendant in the form of double deer (Tang Dynasty)

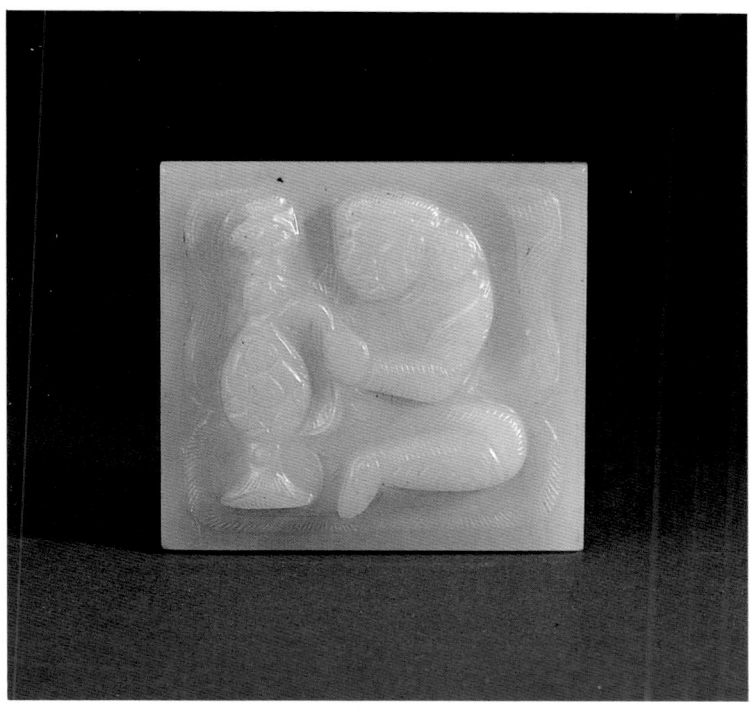

White jade plate with the design of a man holding a pot (Tang Dynasty)

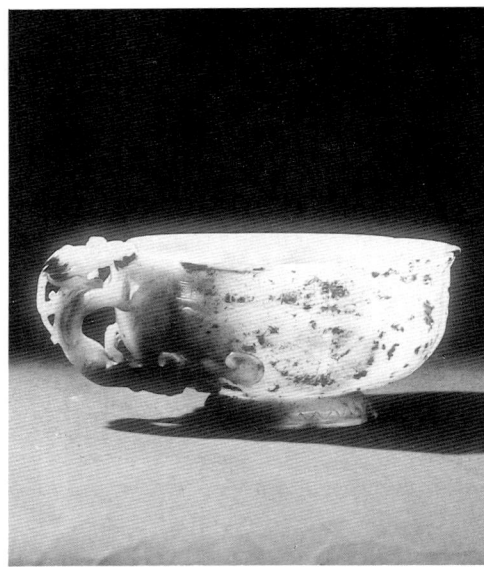

White jade sunflower bowl with dragon design (Song Dynasty)

White jade ornament with openwork design of a hawk picking at a swan (Kin Dynasty)

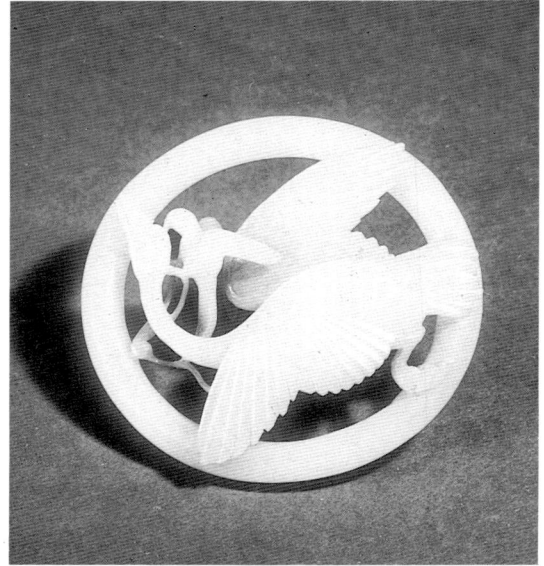

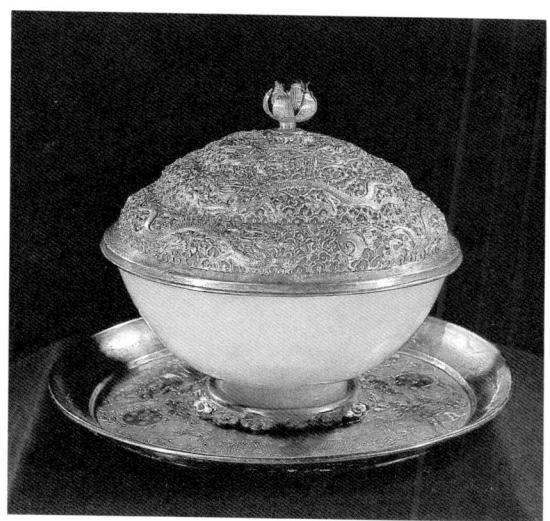

White jade bowl with
gold cover and saucer
(Ming Dynasty)

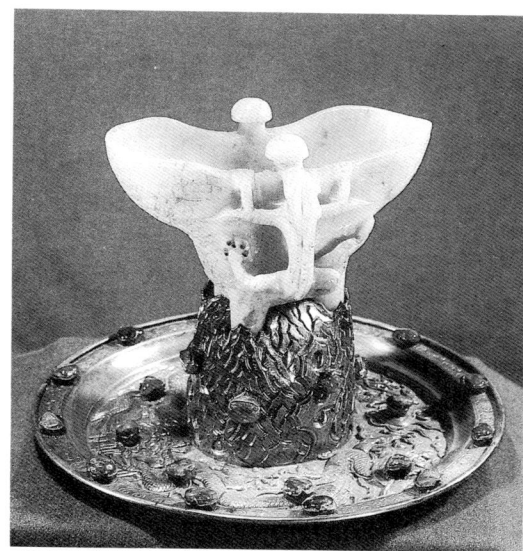

White jade cup on
a gold saucer
(Ming Dynasty)

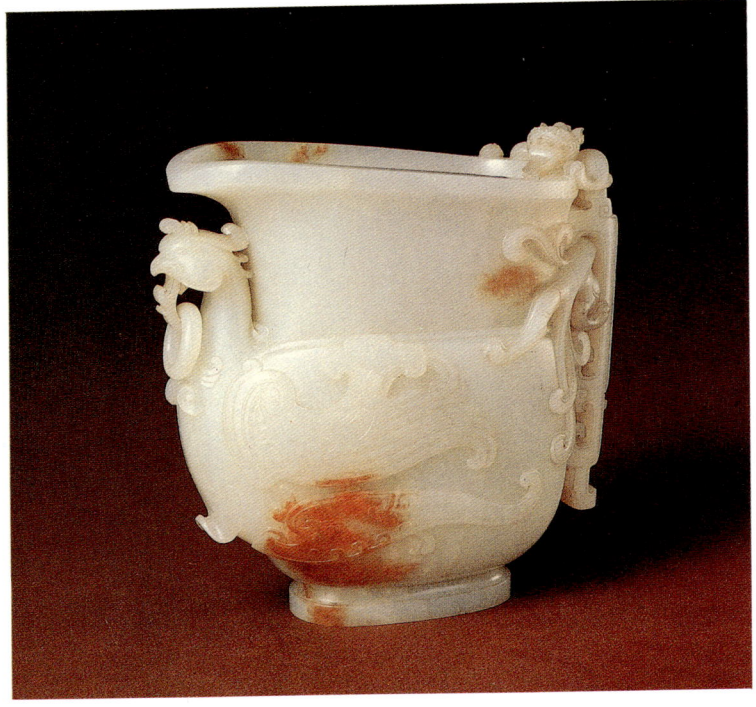

Sapphire wine vessel with phoenix design (Qing Dynasty)

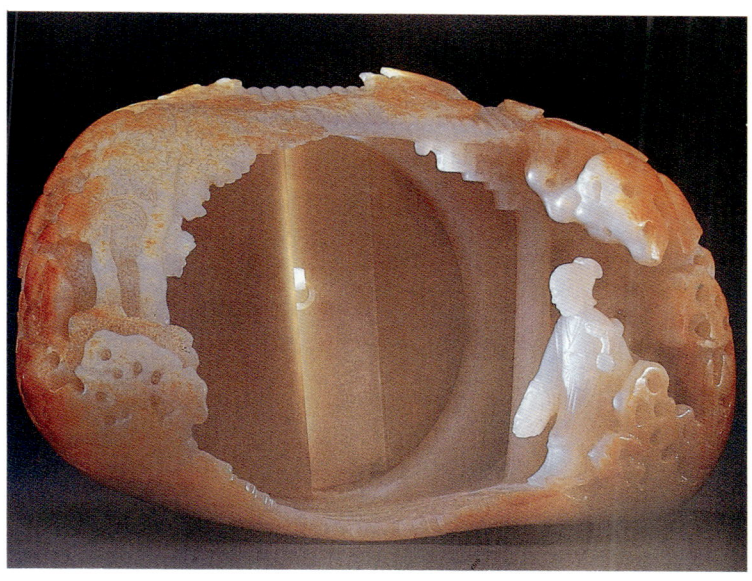

White jade decorative object with the design of a lady (Qing Dynasty)

ture techniques were seen in jade cups and bowls. Dragons, chickens, swans, cranes, ducks, fish, and scenic depictions of "spring mountains" and "autumn rivers" were common themes carved onto jade objects. Imitations of ancient jade works gained popularity. Yuan Dynasty jade showed a particular style of deeply-cut lines.

Great masters of jade carving emerged one after another during the Ming and Qing dynasties, from 1368 to 1911. Lu Zigang, for example, was an artisan particularly skilled at crafting elegant and intricate jade pieces. Of the Qing Dynasty, it could be said that it is the pinnacle of jade carving in China. The artistic style of the periods of Emperor Kangxi and Qianlong demonstrated an achievement unique in history. Imitations of past classics were executed brilliantly. This development had a great deal to do with the fascination and treasuring of jade by the emperors themselves. The white jade cup on a gold saucer and the white bowl on a gold saucer unearthed from the Ming Tombs represented the highest level of craftsmanship of the Ming Dynasty. The single-handled Hotan sapphire wine vessel with phoenix design, the jade wine vessel with dragon and phoenix patterns, and the phoenix-headed agate wine vessel of the Qing Dynasty are known for their fantastic design and superb craftsmanship as creative masterpieces of the period.

A piece of white jade carved with ladies on a hill even more vividly revealed the highly evolved art of jade sculpture during the Qing Dynasty. Six inches high and 10 inches long, the work shows an arched gate leading into a garden where one of the two doors was slightly open. On each side of the gate was a lady. Making use of the original colors of the jade, the sculptor cleverly created a tree casting its branches over the eaves of a house whose pillar was surrounded by rocks. Behind the hill were banana trees under whose shade were stone tables and chairs. Intelligently designed, this work was a masterpiece of realism. The strong three-dimensional effect succeeded in presenting a beautiful garden scene in the southern part of China. Emperor Qianlong was so impressed with it that he wrote a poem which was carved on the side of the work.

## 7. Distinguishing Real from Fake

*W*hat jade lovers are afraid of most are fake jade objects.

In fact, ordinary glass disguised to look like genuine jade is one of the most commonly and most easily manufactured of all fine art imitations. Often seen in the marketplace are small, beautiful-looking and smoothly finished rings, bracelets, and pendants. Just ask the price, and even a layperson can tell they are made from glass molds and are not genuine jade objects. Many glass products are made from molds. When the moulds are fastened together after the high-temperature liquid glass is poured into them, some of the glass will be squeezed out of the edges of the moulds. When it cools, the product will be left with a rough edge which can be felt by hand or discerned with a careful eye. A magnifying glass can often reveal bubbles of air within.

Some glass products are more difficult to examine, especially if their color is similar to the light gray which is a characteristic of jade from Xinjiang. Perhaps careful grinding has removed the rough edges left by the mold process. In such cases, there are three ways of examining these pieces.

First, glass materials are crisp and hard but lack the density and solidity of jade. As a result, they cannot be used with a machine operated or other high-speed grinding tool. Thus, imitation jade made of glass does not bear high relief or rounded sculpture designs.

Second, if even just one air bubble can be found with the help of a magnifying glass, it is a glass reproduction and not genuine jade.

Third, glass, with chromium oxide added, will attain a color similar to that of a ruby; with cobalt oxide, it will appear like sapphire; with chromium and cooper oxides, it will look like emerald. The list goes on. The color of such glass, however, always looks very simple and monochromatic without the smooth, condensed, oily, natural look of real jade.

Interestingly, the imitation jade that has become truly difficult to examine visually are those made of polymer materials. In these cases the color can often be mixed in at will and no bubbles will be visible. Examination under ultraviolet light can immediately give one an answer, but the naked eye must focus on whether the object carries natural stone veins.

When faced with the dire need for jade objects for ritual or sacrificial use, Emperor Taizong of the Tang Dynasty (r. 599-649) issued an edict that small-size jade in square form with a hole in the middle would be made according to the description found in the book *Rituals of the Zhou Dynasty*. For collectors today, what were produced were relics of the Tang Dynasty, but compared with those products made in early periods of Chinese history such as the Zhou or Qin Dynasty, they were viewed as fakes.

The collection of jades in the palaces of the Qing Dynasty was huge and valuable beyond description, yet who would have guessed that among the jade objects offered to the court every year as tributes, many were, in fact, imitation. The emperor himself was not to blame, for the methods for producing imitation jade had by this time become extremely sophisticated.

Another kind of jade commonly called "ancient limestone-like stone" had to go through a firing process so that the surface could obtain a finish whose gray color "appeared to be bones of a boiled chicken."

There was another method invented by a man called Ah Kou from Wuxi during the reign of Emperor Qianlong, which could render dark-colored orange peel creases to new jade products: "Rough jade is mixed with iron residue and hot vinegar. Then, the mixture is placed on damp soil for a dozen days before being buried underground for several months. This way, the jade will acquire a dusty gray finish which will not easily fade. The result is that they appear to be antique jade."

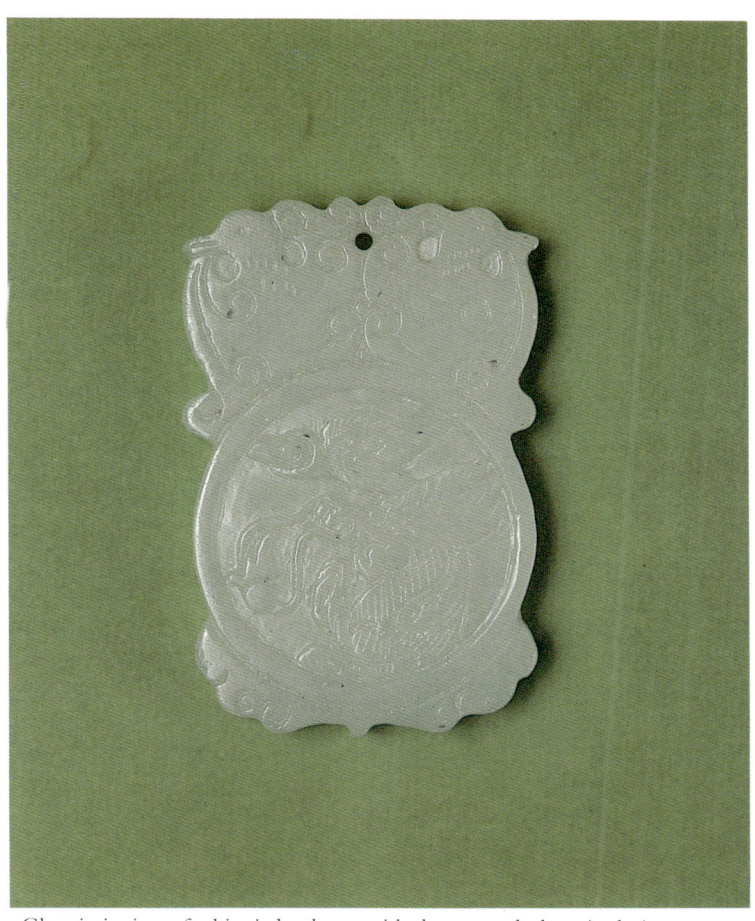

Glass imitation of white jade plaque with dragon and phoenix design
(contemporary)

## 8. For the Collector

$\mathcal{J}$ade is synonymous with elegance, luxury, and extremely high monetary value. Many museums throughout the world feature well known, priceless jade treasures. Does this mean that collecting jade is beyond the ability of most individuals? Not so. Collecting jade does not always have to mean paying high prices.

The collection of jade relies heavily on favorable economic conditions. While it is practically impossible to consider museum-quality pieces, those with particularly strong economic means can follow most international auctions or art dealers. Those with slightly less robust economic means can collect jade according to historical eras, such as the Tang, Song, Ming, and Qing dynasties. Or they can follow the categories of the purpose and functions of jade, such as ancient jade pendants, ritual jade, and mountain jade. It is also possible to collect jade according to subject categories such as square jade with a hole in the middle, round jade with a hole in the middle, jade birds, jade dragons, jade human figurines, jade cups, and jade belt buckles, etc.

In China, collectors at this level can only find their objects in antique stores or at auctions, as what they are looking for are all classified as cultural relics. Where conditions permit, they may go and find what they want in antique stores and auction outside mainland China, where there are often unexpected amounts of ancient Chinese jade of surprisingly high quality. In a book entitled *One Hundred Pieces of Jade from the Mountain Villa of Lantian* by Deng Shuping, many of these pieces of ancient jade are not only of top quality but some are even considered priceless national treasures, very rarely seen even inside China.

As for the ranks of collectors new to the world of jade, pendants are generally considered to be the best starting point. Pieces with themes of good luck symbols, flowers, birds, and figures of the Buddha offer a wide selection, partly because of their relatively large quantity and relative similarity in price. The standards for such collections are exquisite workmanship, fine initial quality, nice colors, and unique or rare shapes. Since the techniques of jade craftsmen vary greatly, however, it is often possible to discover many outstanding pieces whose price may be several times higher than other seemingly similar pieces.

In China, state-owned cultural relic stores are manned by qualified staff members, having an authentic channel of supply, and therefore are almost entirely free from imitation jade. The opening up of state warehouses in recent years has allowed the some specially-permitted real antiques to be sold to private buyers.

Good jade occasionally turns up at auction where highly-trained appraisers oversee all pieces to ensure their quality.

State-owned art stores and jewelry shops normally only carry new jade pieces and there is no concealment of the jade's true identity. It may indeed be genuine but it is not antique and will not be represented as such. Trading here is fair and the procedures are standard and secure to ensure piece of mind on behalf of the buyer.

According to Chinese law concerning cultural relics and antiquities, no markets dealing in art objects are allowed to deal in cultural relics. What this means is that most of the so-called "antique jade" being sold in such markets are likely to be antique in style only and are not believed to be genuine. Even if such a piece was determined to be genuine, purchasing such a piece would likely result in a heavy fine or other punishment for the buyer.

In the marketplace, genuine jade will be in the form of pendants, bracelets, and objects of jadeite. There are also small but exquisitely sculpted pieces of white or yellow soapstone, Xinjiang jade, as well as bracelets and Dushan jade. As a general rule, always check the price. If it looks too good to be true, it probably is.

In recent years, there are many antique markets at tourist spots in China. But most of the "antiques" that you find on these markets are fake ones. If you are a specialist or you are accompanied by a specialist, you may find a really good and genuine piece.

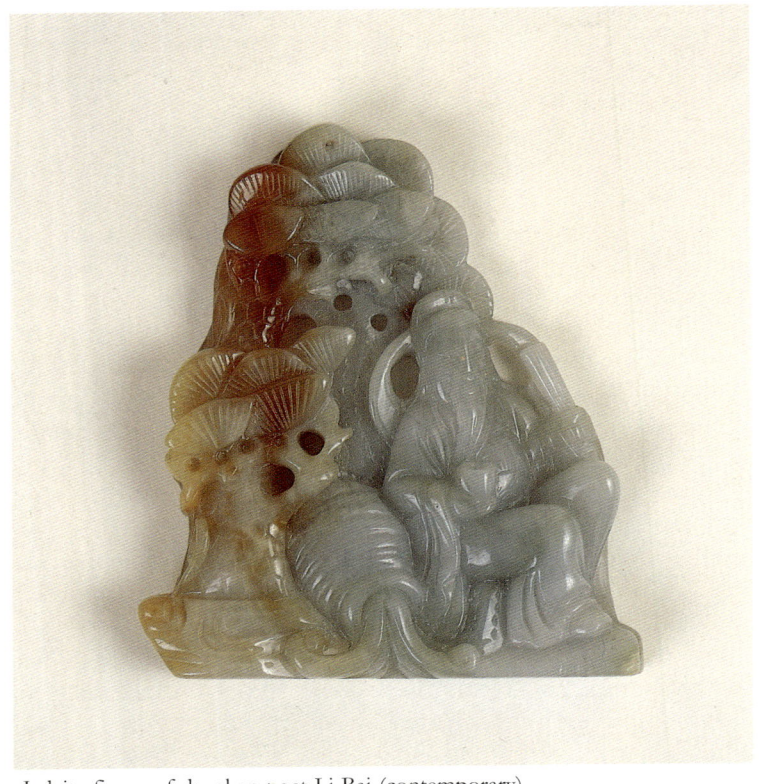

Jadeite figure of drunken poet Li Bai (contemporary)

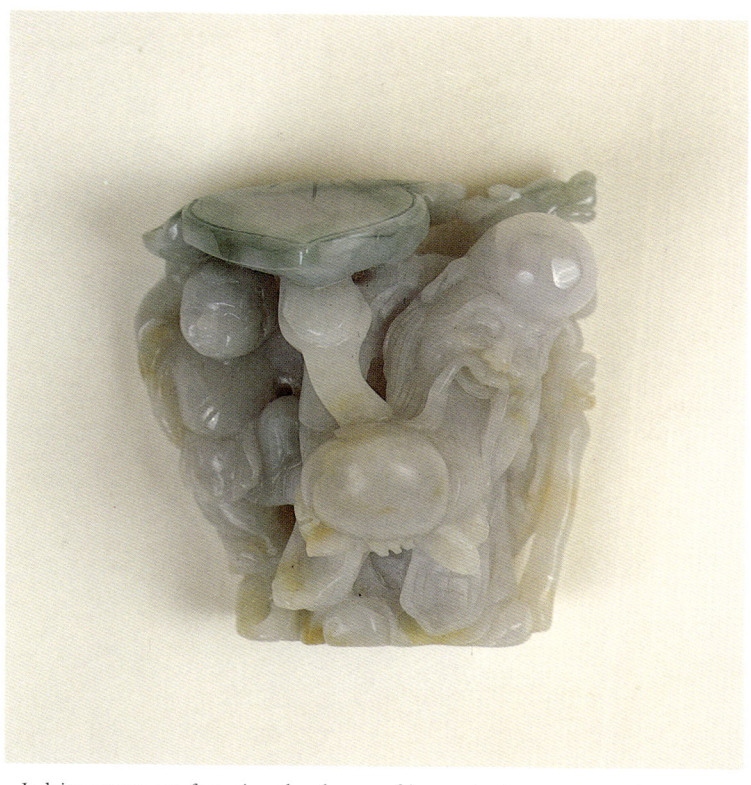

Jadeite ornament featuring the theme of longevity (contemporary)

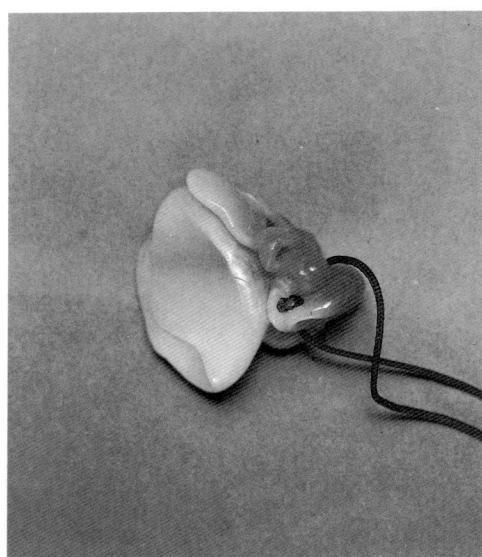

White jade pendant of
lotus and fish
(contemporary)

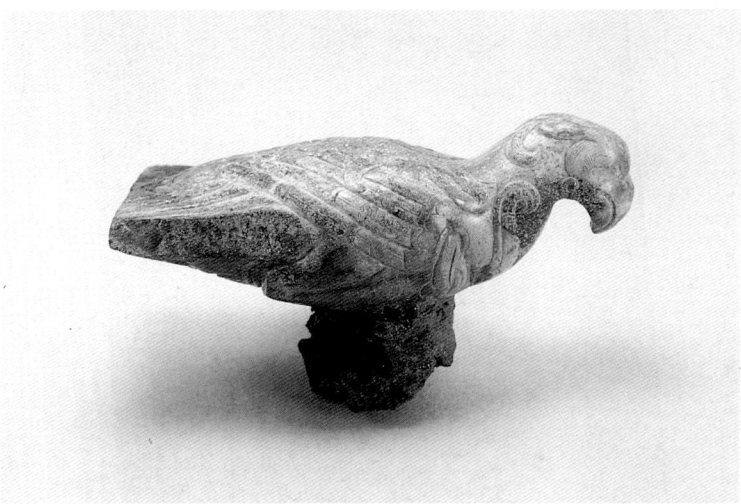

Jade walking stick handle in the form of a turtledove (Warring States Period)

Sapphire and white jade
pendant with figure design
(contemporary)

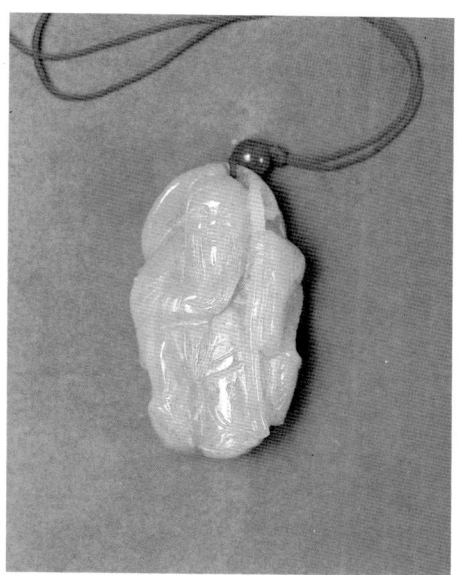

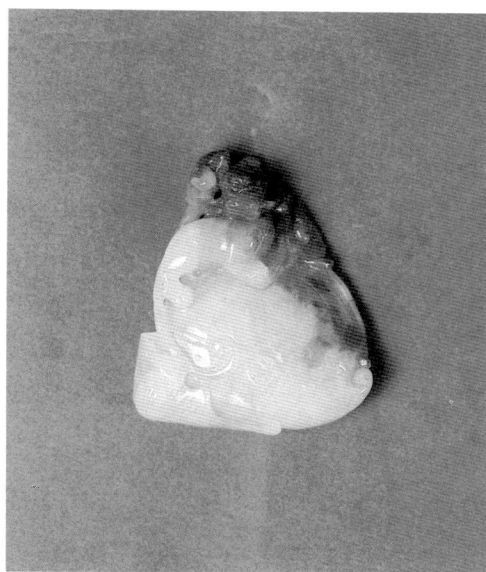

Jadeite pendant
featuring the theme of
happiness and longevity
(contemporary)

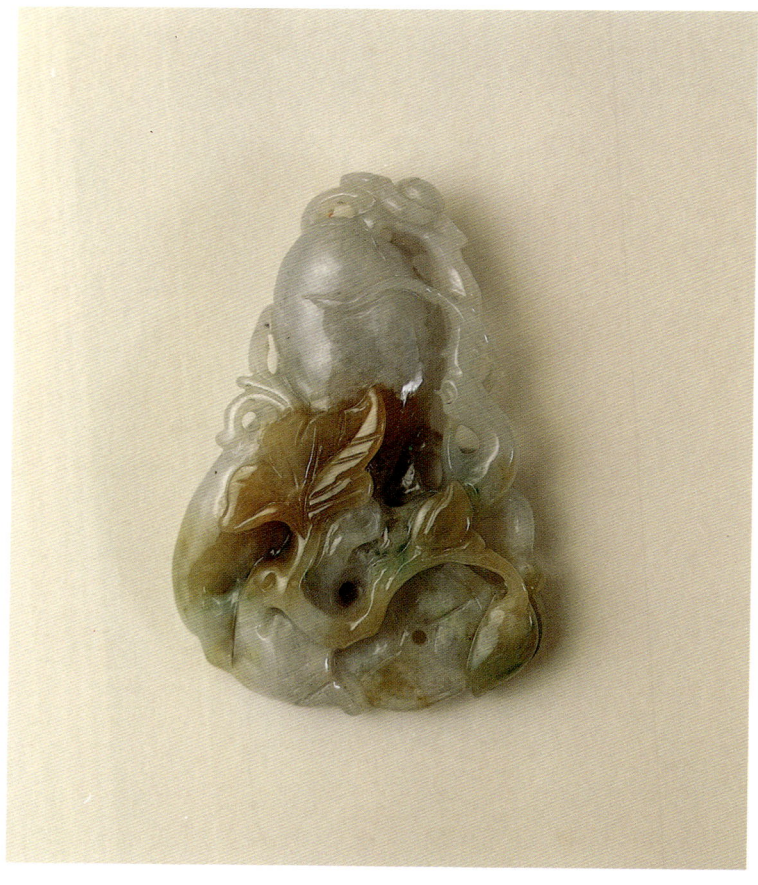

Jadeite pendant with vegetable and fruit designs (contemporary)

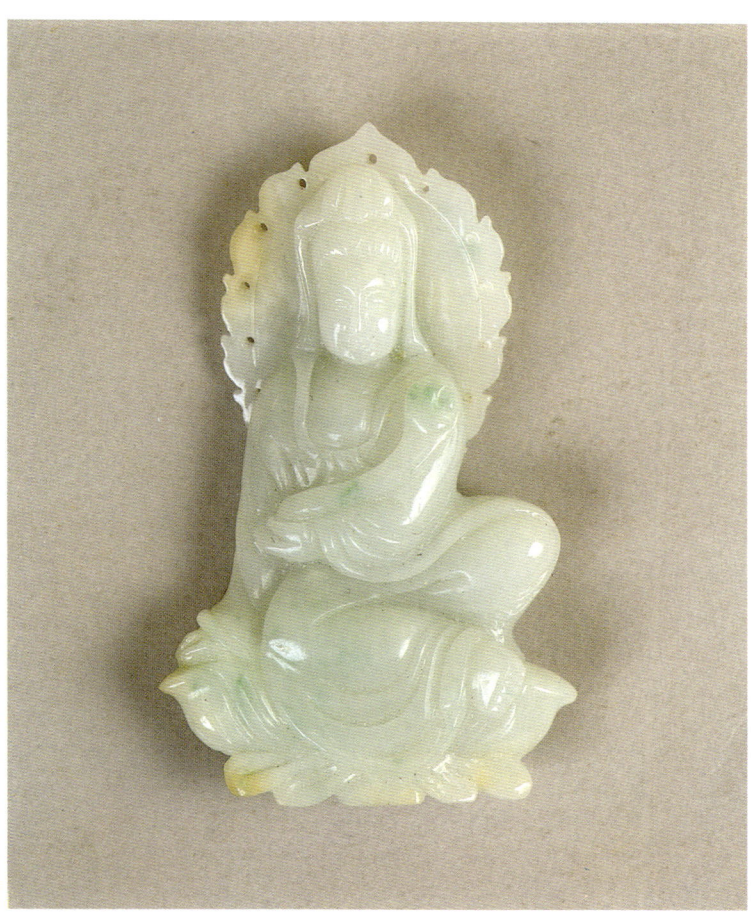

Jadeite *Guanyin*, or Goddess of Mercy (contemporary)

## 9. The Assessment of Jade

*T*he appraisal of jade is conducted according to the two categories of jade: new jade and old jade. The emphasis in the appraisal of new jade focuses on the level of the quality of raw jade and the technical skill of the artisan. The appraisal of old jade is much more complicated. Apart from the basic requirements above, when assessing old jade, attention must be given to the historical era and history and function of the specific piece.

The value of jade objects is built on clear delineation of the historical eras in which they were created and used. Without a clear definition of the time the object was made, there is no way to discuss its value with any accuracy. To give appraisal to a piece of old jade requires years of expert knowledge in art history, as well as social and cultural history. Because China did not engage in formal archaeological studies for a long period of time, the appraisal of jade without the reference of already-unearthed objects was based purely on heuristic methodologies and hard-earned practical experiences. As a result, people cherished their new discoveries to such an extent that they rarely passed onto others the skill gained from experience in telling the roundness of a fish eye or the length of a dragon claw. In the last few decades, however, this situation has changed.

Due to the fact that some jade objects have survived for thousands of years from one family member to the next, it was not unusual, for example, to find a piece of jade in a tomb which may have in fact been several hundred years older than the occupant of the tomb itself.

There were often similarities in the styles and characteristics of jade objects made toward the end of one historical period and those made in the beginning of the following historical period. For example, a typical jade piece, round in shape, with a hole in the middle carrying double-tail dragon designs have been unearthed from tombs of both the Warring States Period and the Han Dynasty. The thin jade tablet in the form of a semicircle from the Songze culture dating back to over 5,000 years ago was discovered again in a tomb of the Liangzhu Culture 1,000 years later. It is reasonable to say that the one piece unearthed from the Liangzhu tomb might have been a relic of the earlier Songze Culture. This was because both cultures existed in the same region and archaeologists generally believe that the Liangzhu Culture developed from the Songze Culture. It is also not wrong to assume that such a piece was a product of the Liangzhu Culture, for it was found from a tomb of the period and the traces of cutting bore witness to the soft sculpting techniques common to both cultures.

In assessing jade, one has to learn to make a comprehensive analysis, apart from mastering their distinctive styles of different historical periods. Take the jade dragon for example. Jade dragons dating from prehistory to the Ming and Qing dynasties all can be considered as one category, but careful comparative study of every piece and part on the body of the jade dragons from different periods of history reveals a highly complex set of criteria. For instance, the evolution in the form of the dragon's eyes, horns, feet, claws, scales and tail should all be considered.

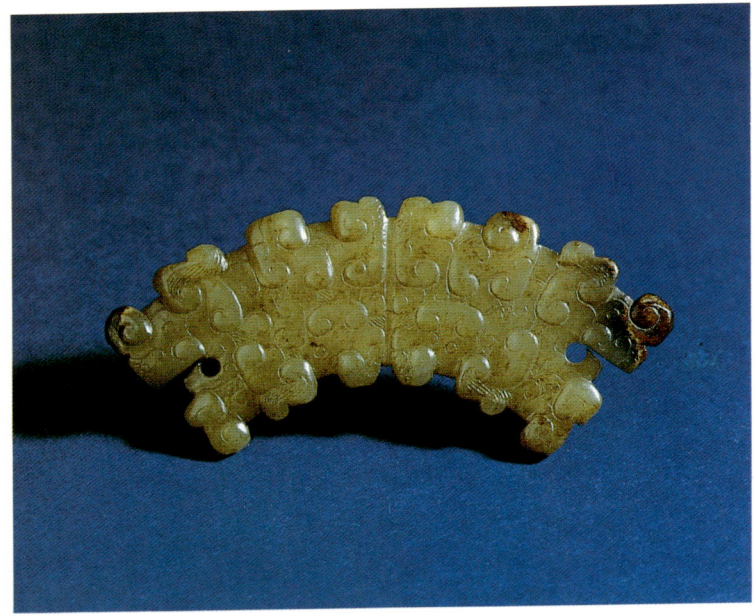

White jade pendant with dragon design (Spring and Autumn Period)

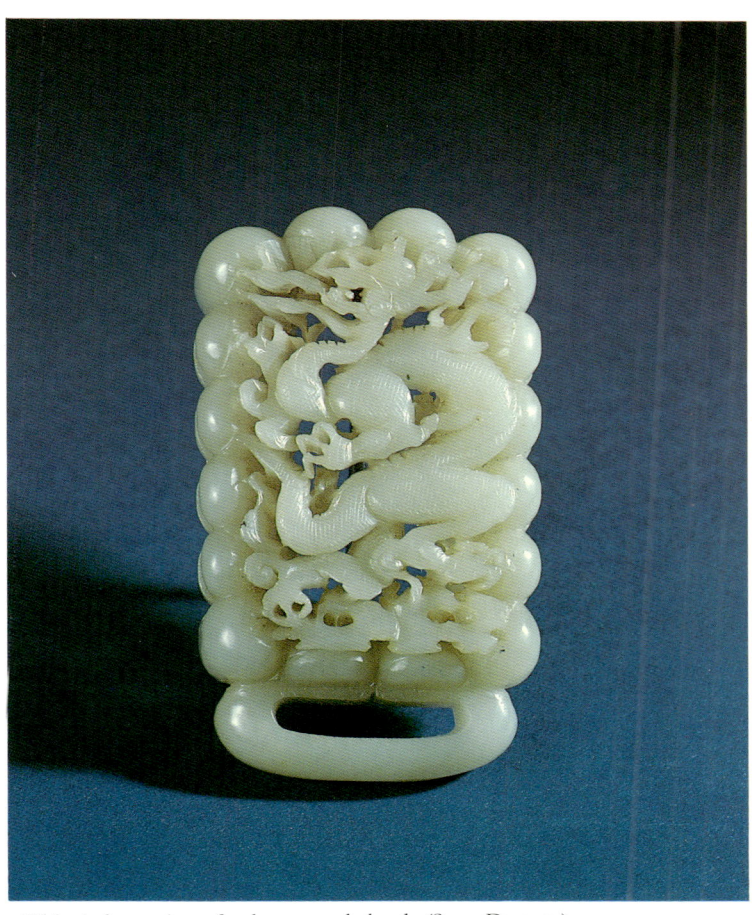

White jade carving of a dragon and clouds (Song Dynasty)

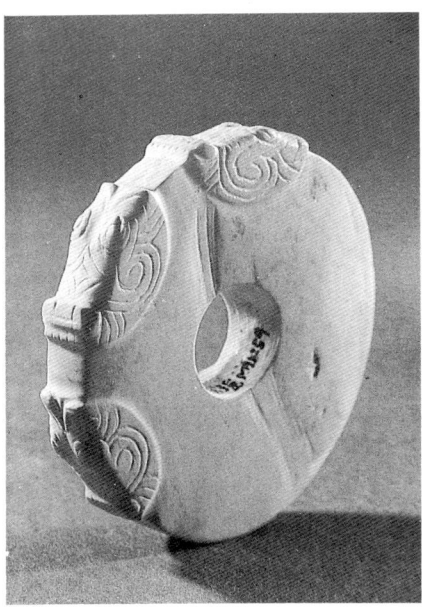

A round jade with a hole in the middle with the design of dragon head (Liangzhu Culture)

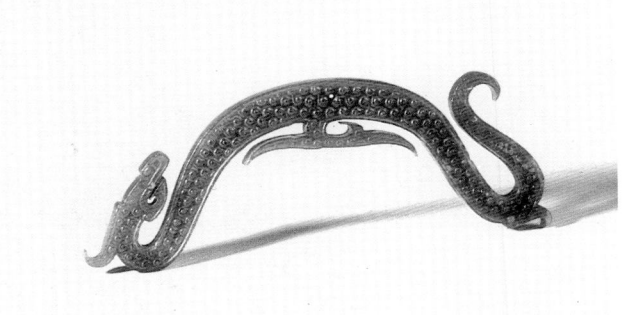

Sapphire dragon-design pendant (Warring States Period)

Round jade with a hole in the middle carved with double-tail dragon design (Warring States Period-Han Dynasty)

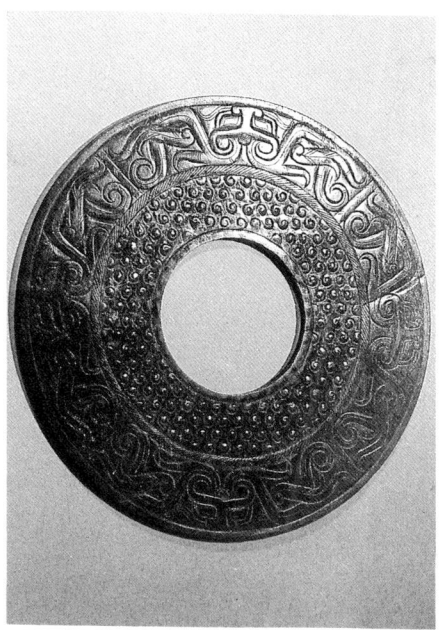

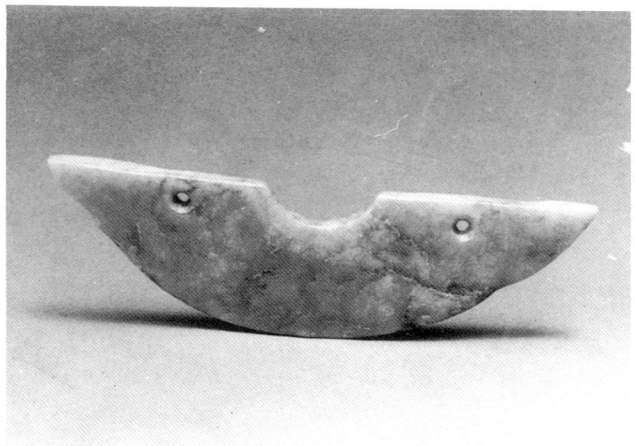

Jade tablet in the shape of a bridge (Songze-Liangzhu Cultures)

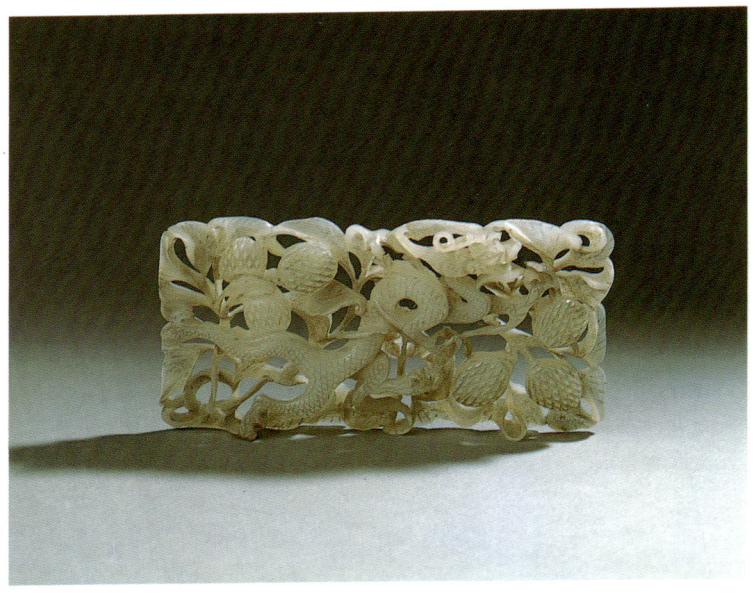

Celadon ink box with openwork design (Yuan Dynasty)

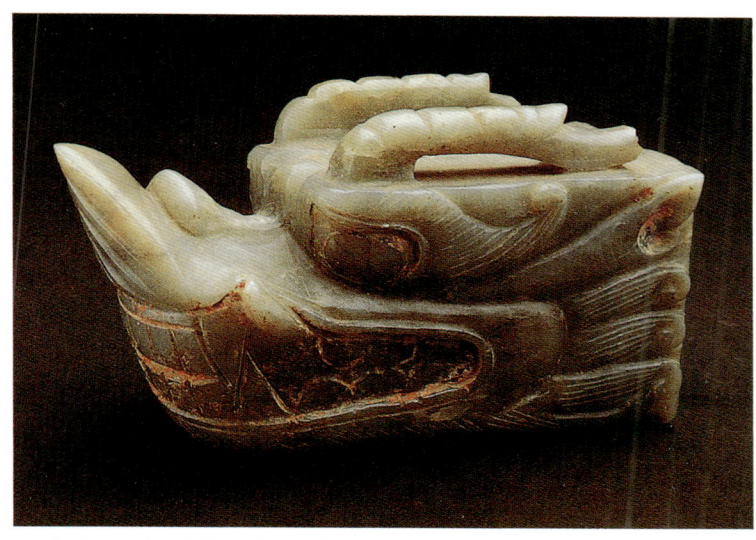

Jade dragon head (Liao Dynasty)

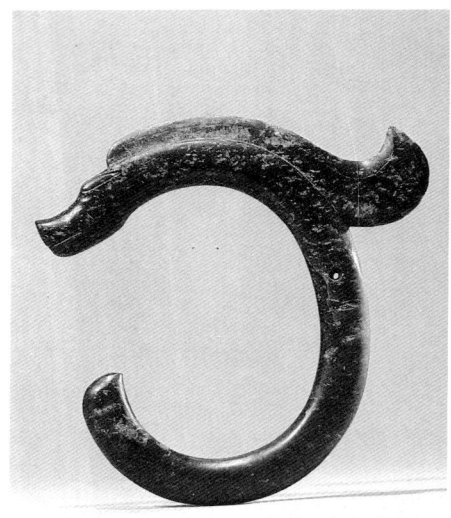

Jade dragon (Hongshan Culture)

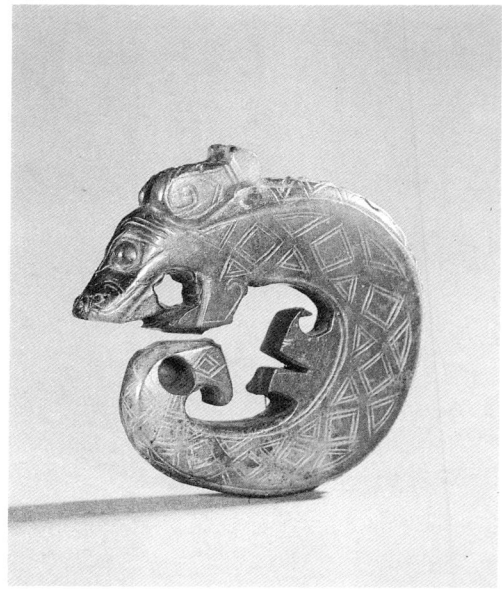

Jade dragon
(Shang Dynasty)

Jade vase with dragon
design (Qing Dynasty)

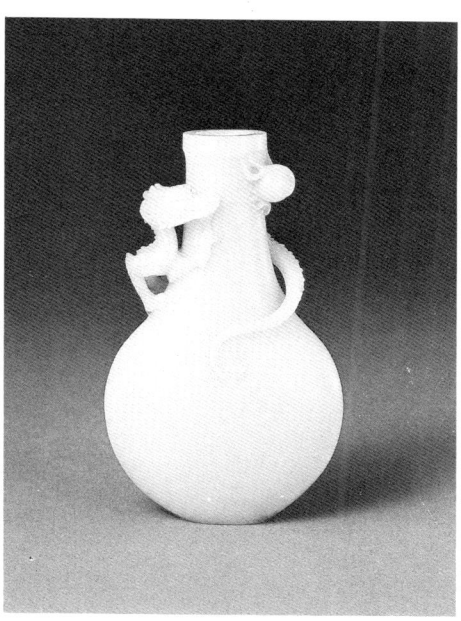

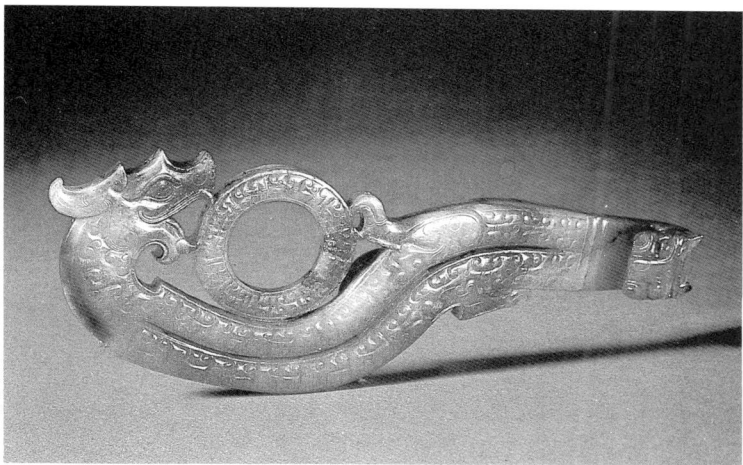

Jade belt buckle with dragon and tiger designs (Western Han Dynasty)

74

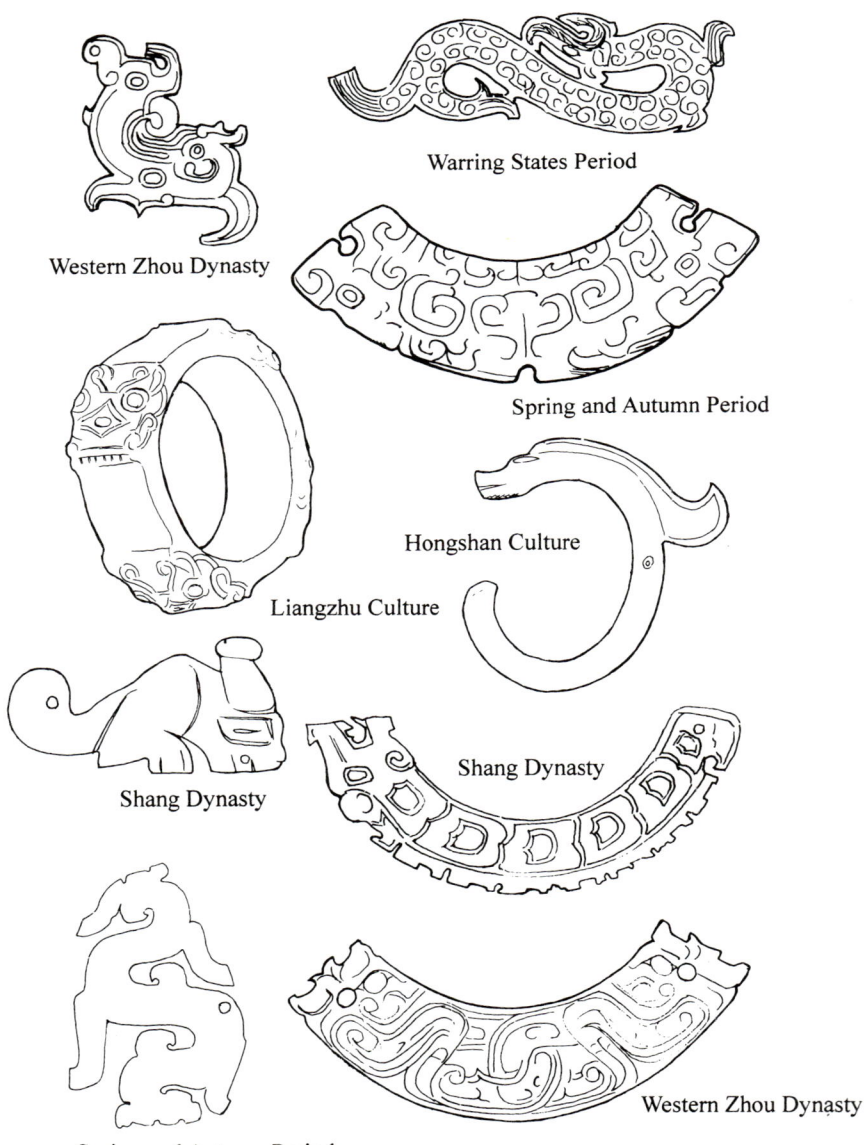

Warring States Period

Western Zhou Dynasty

Spring and Autumn Period

Hongshan Culture

Liangzhu Culture

Shang Dynasty

Shang Dynasty

Western Zhou Dynasty

Spring and Autumn Period

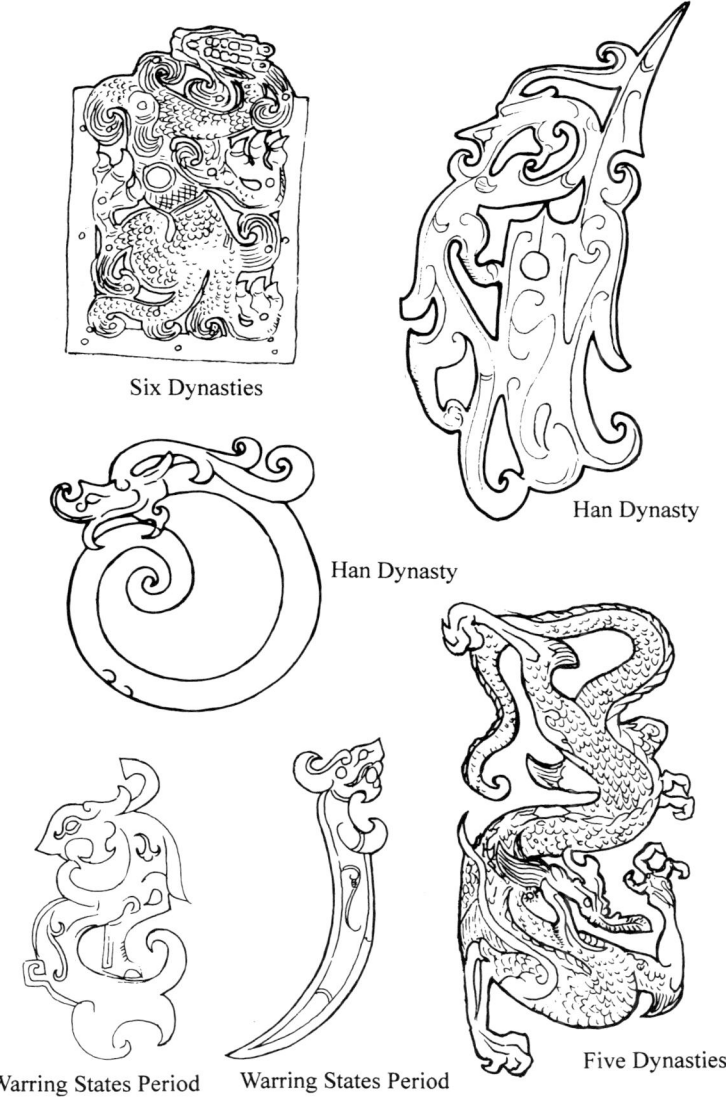

Six Dynasties

Han Dynasty

Han Dynasty

Warring States Period

Warring States Period

Five Dynasties

76

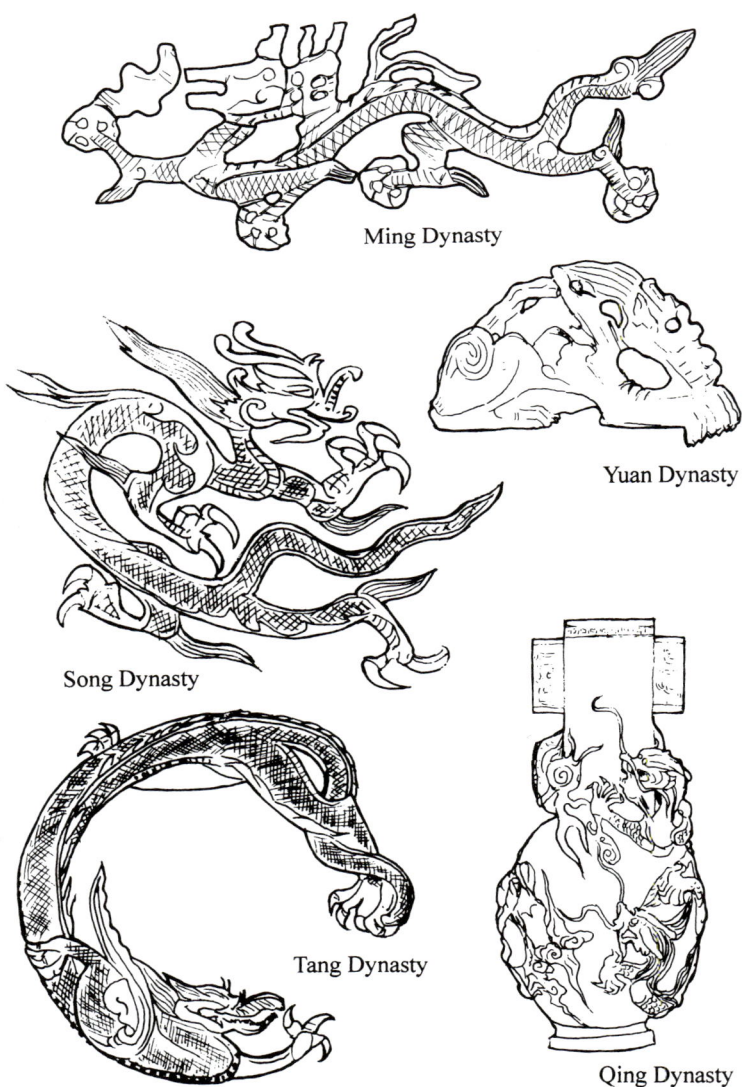

Ming Dynasty

Yuan Dynasty

Song Dynasty

Tang Dynasty

Qing Dynasty

# Chronological Table of Chinese Dynasties

| | |
|---|---|
| Five August Emperors | c.30th-21st century B.C. |
| Xia Dynasty | c.21st-16th century B.C. |
| Shang Dynasty | c.16th-11th century B.C. |
| Zhou Dynasty | c.11th century-221 B.C. |
|   Western Zhou Dynasty | c.11th century-771 B.C. |
|   Eastern Zhou Dynasty | 770-256 B.C. |
|     Spring and Autumn Period | 770-476 B.C. |
|     Warring States Period | 475-221 B.C. |
| Qin Dynasty | 221-207 B.C. |
| Han Dynasty | 206 B.C.-A.D. 220 |
|   Western Han Dynasty | 206 B.C.-A.D. 23 |
|   Eastern Han Dynasty | A.D. 25-220 |
| Three Kingdoms Period | 220-280 |
| Jin Dynasty | 265-420 |
|   Western Jin Dynasty | 265-316 |
|   Eastern Jin Dynasty | 317-420 |
| Southern and Northern Dynasties | 420-589 |
| Sui Dynasty | 581-618 |
| Tang Dynasty | 618-907 |
| Five Dynasties | 907-960 |
| Song Dynasty | 960-1279 |
|   Northern Song Dynasty | 960-1127 |
|   Southern Song Dynasty | 1127-1279 |
| Liao Dynasty | 916-1125 |
| Kin Dynasty | 1115-1234 |
| Yuan Dynasty | 1271-1368 |
| Ming Dynasty | 1368-1644 |
| Qing Dynasty | 1644-1911 |

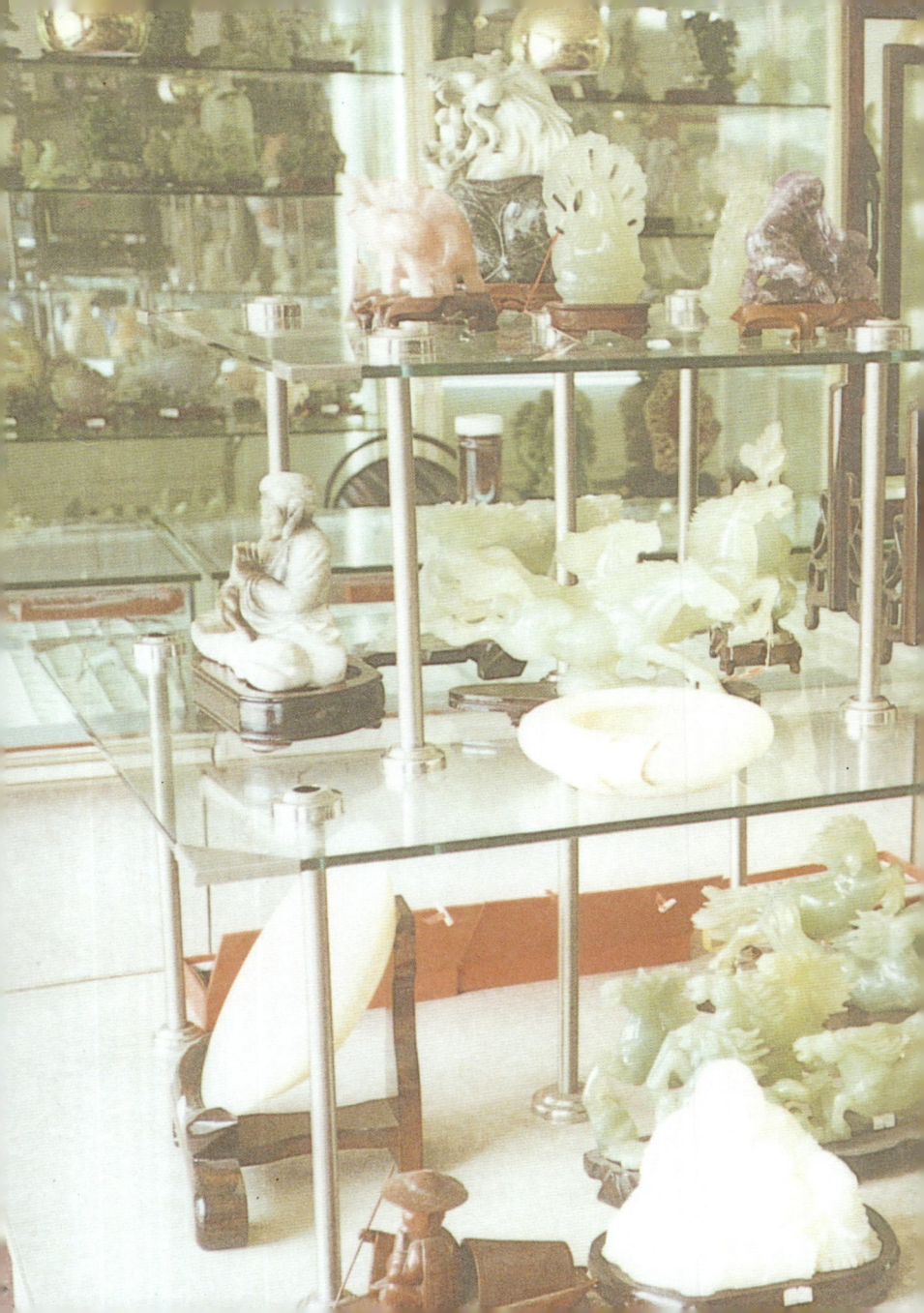